NEVER REVOKED

NOSTRA AETATE AS ONGOING CHALLENGE FOR JEWISH-CHRISTIAN DIALOGUE

Louvain Theological and Pastoral Monographs is a publishing venture whose purpose is to provide those involved in pastoral ministry throughout the world with studies inspired by Louvain's long tradition of theological excellence within the Roman Catholic tradition. The volumes selected for publication in the series are expected to express some of today's finest reflection on current theology and pastoral practice.

Members of the Editorial Board

LOUVAIN THEOLOGICAL & PASTORAL MONOGRAPHS
——————————— 40 ———————————

NEVER REVOKED

Nostra Aetate as Ongoing Challenge
for Jewish-Christian Dialogue

edited by

Marianne Moyaert & Didier Pollefeyt

PEETERS
LEUVEN – PARIS – WALPOLE, MA

WILLIAM B. EERDMANS PUBLISHING COMPANY
GRAND RAPIDS, MICHIGAN/CAMBRIDGE, U.K.

2010

Copyright (c) 2010 by
Peeters Publishers, and
William B. Eerdmans Publishing Company
All rights reserved

Published jointly 2010
in Belgium by
Peeters Publishers
Bondgenotenlaan 153
3000 Leuven
and in the United States of America by
Wm. B. Eerdmans Publishing Company
2140 Oak Industrial Dr. N.E., Grand Rapids, Michigan 49505 /
P.O. Box 163 Cambridge CB3 9PU U.K.
www.eerdmans.com

Manufactured in Belgium

12   11   10   09   08   5   4   3   2   1

A catalogue record for this book is available from the Library of Congress

Eerdmans ISBN 978-0-8028-6571-7
Peeters ISBN 978-90-429-2236-5
D/2010/0602/35

TABLE OF CONTENTS

THE COVENANT NEVER REVOKED
REMEMBERING THE CONCILIAR COURAGE
TO DIALOGUE

Marianne MOYAERT & Didier POLLEFEYT

The Declaration *Nostra Aetate* issued by the Second Vatican Council on October 28, 1965, on 'the relationship of the Church to non-Christian religions' marks a revolutionary "milestone"[1] in the history of interreligious relations. Indeed, *Nostra Aetate* expresses a conversion of the Catholic Church towards other religions and Judaism in particular. With this document the Catholic Church sought to establish a new climate in which encounter and dialogue were understood as part of the Church's role in the world. As such, *Nostra Aetate* expresses the dialogical spirit of the Second Vatican Council, whose "intention it was to rally the highest possible majority on the council floor in favor of a change of attitude of Christians and the Church toward the members of other religions."[2]

In the opening chapter of this book, Mathijs Lamberigts and Leo Declerck remark quite rightly, that "the presentation and approval of a positive text on relations with the Jews was actually far from evident."[3] Not only could the Church expect objections from the Arab world. It soon became clear that within the Catholic world there were

---

[1] Commission for Religious Relations with the Jews, *Guidelines and Suggestions for Implementing the Conciliar Declaration 'Nostra Aetate' (n.4).*

[2] Jacques Dupuis, *Christianity and the Religions: From Confrontation to Dialogue* (London: Darton, Longman & Todd, 2002) 59.

[3] Mathijs Lamberigts and Leo Declerck, "Vatican II on the Jews: A Historical Survey," in this volume, 13-56, 16.

also theologians and bishops not altogether that enthusiastic about the conciliar intention to prepare a document on Judaism. That the Second Vatican Council addressed the Church's relations with the Jews at all was due in large measure to two individuals: Pope John XXIII and Cardinal Augustine Bea. They demonstrated boldness and perseverance in setting Jewish-Christian relations on the conciliar agenda. Rabbi David Meyer is likewise struck by the courageous spirit that animated the writers of the document.[4] They not only had the courage "to reflect on the [Church's] share of responsibility" in the *Shoah,* they also had the resolution to rethink, re-interpret and change some of the Church's teaching regarding Jews and Judaism. *Nostra Aetate* # 4 acknowledges that for nearly two thousand years the relations between the Church and the Jewish people were marked by ignorance and confrontation, and expresses the hope to change the future for the better. It confirms the strong bond between the Church and the Jewish people and provides an opportunity to further the dialogue between Jews and Christians. *Nostra Aetate* "encouraged Christians to renounce the old anti-Judaism completely and to grow from apologia to encounter, from considering Jews as objects of contempt to respecting them as subjects of faith."[5]

After the Second Vatican Council, Pope Paul VI (1963-1978), and especially John Paul II showed the same tenacity and dialogical spirit which inspired *Nostra Aetate.* John Paul II (1978-2005) often devoted his energy to improving relations between Jews and Catholics. During his pontificate the Church condemned anti-Semitism, reflected on the roots of Christian anti-Judaic attitudes

---

[4] David Meyer, *"Nostra Aetate*: Past, Present, Future: A Jewish Perspective," in this volume, 117-132.

[5] Didier Pollefeyt, "Jews and Christians after Auschwitz: From Substitution to Interreligious Dialogue," *Jews and Christians: Rivals or Partners for the Kingdom of God? In Search of an Alternative for the Theology of Substitution,* ed. Didier Pollefeyt (Louvain: Peeters, 1997) 10-37, 21.

and prayed for the forgiveness of sins committed by "some sons and daughters of the Church"[6] during the Holocaust. In many evocative symbolic actions John Paul II expressed his personal commitment to Jewish-Christian dialogue. He affirmed both in words and deeds that the Jewish people is the "chosen and beloved people of God, the people of God's covenant which due to God's faithfulness is never broken and is still alive."[7] In connection with this, we recall his address in Rome on October 31, 1997, where John Paul II discussed God's election of Israel: "This people [of Israel] is assembled and led by Yahweh, creator of heaven and of earth. Its existence is therefore not purely a fact of nature or of culture in the sense that the resourcefulness proper to one's nature is expressed in culture. It is a supernatural fact. This people perseveres despite everything because it is the people of the covenant, and despite human infidelities, Yahweh is faithful to his covenant. To ignore this most basic principle is to adopt a Marcionism against which the church immediately and vigorously reacted, conscious of a vital link with the Old Testament, without which the New Testament itself is emptied of meaning."[8] Time and again, Pope John Paul II expressed that the relation between Church and Israel no longer stands under the sign of divorce, but rather reflects the strong bond between the people of the first and second covenant. Perhaps one of the strongest expressions of this belief are his words

[6] Commission for Religious Relations with the Jews, "We Remember: A Reflection on the Shoah." www.vatican.va.

[7] Walter Kasper, "Paths Taken and Enduring Questions in Jewish-Christian Relations Today: Thirty Years of the Commission for Religious Relations with the Jews," *The Catholic Church and the Jewish People: Recent Reflections from Rome*, ed. Phillip A. Cunningham, Norbert J. Hofmann and Joseph Sievers (New York: Fordham University Press, 2007) 3-11, 6.

[8] John Paul II, Address in Rome on October 31, 1977. Cited in Avery Dulles, "The Covenant with Israel," *First Things: Journal of Religion, Culture and Public Life*, November 2005; www.firstthings.com.

that the "covenant" is "never revoked (Rom 11:29)."[9] Israel is and remains God's chosen and beloved people, even if it can not accept Jesus as the promised Messiah.

Through his personal commitment to the improvement of Jewish-Christian relations and the way he 'embodied' the dialogical spirit of *Nostra Aetate*, John Paul II has made the necessary room for further theological reflection on interreligious dialogue in general, and the precise nature of the relation between Israel and the Church in particular. The release of the document, *Reflections on Covenant and Mission* (2002),[10] issued by the Ecumenical and Interreligious Affairs Committee of the United States Conference of Catholic Bishops and the National Council of Synagogues USA, marks a significant step forward in Jewish-Christian dialogue. It was the result of more than two decades of interreligious discussions between leaders of both Jewish and Catholic communities in the United States and contains both Jewish and Catholic reflections on God's call to both peoples. The Catholic reflections describe "the growing respect for the Jewish tradition that has unfolded since the Second Vatican Council. A deepening Catholic appreciation of the eternal covenant between God and the Jewish people, together with a recognition of a divinely-given mission to Jews to witness to God's faithful love, lead to the conclusion that campaigns that target Jews for conversion to Christianity are no longer theologically acceptable in the Catholic Church."[11] This document deepens theological reflection on the relation between

[9] Pope John Paul II affirmed the lasting meaning of Israel and the 'Never Revoked Covenant' in his speech for the Jewish community of Mainz, West-Germany, on November 17, 1980.

[10] Cf. Bishops' Committee on Ecumenical and Interreligious Affairs and the National Council of Synagogues, "Reflections on Covenant and Mission," *Origins* 32 (2002) 218-224.

[11] Bishops' Committee on Ecumenical and Interreligious Affairs and the National Council of Synagogues, "Reflections on Covenant and Mission," 219.

the Church and Israel and takes the dialogue between Judaism and Christianity another step forward. However, other steps are still needed. Now that the pontificate of John Paul II has come to an end, the question is, how is his successor, Benedict XVI relating to the heritage of *Nostra Aetate*? Will he be prepared to further develop some of the burning theological issues?

The fact that Pope Benedict XVI began his papacy with already some track record in Jewish-Catholic dialogue is promising.[12] As Cardinal Ratzinger, he tried to develop a theology of Jewish-Christian relations. Consider, for instance, the document *The Jewish People and the Holy Scriptures in the Christian Bible* (2001) by the Pontifical Biblical Commission, which was authorized by Cardinal Joseph Ratzinger. This document stresses the continuing importance of the Torah for Christians. Ratzinger, who penned the document's introduction, expresses his hope "to advance the dialogue between Christians and Jews with clarity and in a spirit of mutual esteem and affection."[13] We should also mention two of his articles, 'The Heritage of Abraham: The Gift of Christmas'[14] and 'Interreligious Dialogue and Jewish Christian Relations'[15]. Both were later published in Ratzinger's book, *Many Religions – One Covenant: Israel, the Church and the World*, which comments positively on the reconciliation among Jews and Christians, and emphasizes the lasting role of the Jewish people.[16]

---

[12] Unpublished lecture by prof. J. T. Pawlikowski at St. Paul's University, Ottawa, Canada, on October 30, 2008.

[13] Pontifical Biblical Commission, *The Jewish People and the Holy Scriptures in the Christian Bible*, Rome, 2001; www.vatican.va.

[14] Cardinal Joseph Ratzinger, "The Heritage of Abraham, the Gift of Christmas," *L'Osservatore Romano*, 29 December 2000.

[15] Ratzinger, "Interreligious Dialogue and Jewish-Christian Relations," *Communio* 25 (1998) 29-41.

[16] Ratzinger, *Many Religions – One Covenant: Israel, the Church, and the World* (San Francisco, CA: Ignatius Press, 1999) 103.

Ratzinger has always considered Jewish-Catholic relations as *sui generis* and this remained obvious even when commencing his pontificate as Pope Benedict XVI. Indeed, shortly after his election, he affirmed the doctrinal legacy of *Nostra Aetate* and expressed his will to continue fostering good pastoral relations with the Jewish people. He aims to emulate the example of his predecessor with the same intention to reach out to the Jewish people. On June 9, 2005, less than two months into his pontificate, Pope Benedict XVI addressed a delegation of the International Jewish Committee on Interreligious Consultations, declaring that Vatican II "affirmed the Church's conviction that, in the mystery of the divine election, the beginnings of her faith are already to be found in Abraham, Moses and the Prophets ... At the very beginning of my Pontificate, I wish to assure you that the Church remains firmly committed, in her catechesis and in every aspect of her life, to implementing this decisive teaching." Pope Benedict XVI then continued with emphasis, "In the years following the Council, my predecessors Pope Paul VI and, in a particular way, Pope John Paul II, took significant steps towards improving relations with the Jewish people. *It is my intention to continue on this path.*"[17]

In a letter to Cardinal Walter Kasper, President of the Holy See's Commission on Religious Relations with the Jews, on October 26, 2005, the day prior to the Vatican's official commemoration of the fortieth anniversary of Vatican II's *Nostra Aetate*, Benedict XVI affirmed "his determination to walk in the footsteps traced by my beloved predecessor Pope John Paul II."[18] In his address in Cologne on the occasion of his visit to the Synagogue, he refers to

[17] http://www.bc.edu/research/cjl/.

[18] Letter of His Holiness Benedict XVI to the President of the Commission of Religious Relations with the Jews on the Occasion of the 40th Anniversary of the Declaration *Nostra Aetate*, www.vatican.va.

Nostra Aetate # 4, recalling the common roots and the immensely rich spiritual heritage that Jews and Christians share.

> With Saint Paul, Christians are convinced that "the gifts and the call of God are irrevocable" (Rom 11:29, cf. 9:6,11; 11:1ff.). In considering the Jewish roots of Christianity (cf. Rom 11:16-24), my venerable Predecessor, quoting a statement by the German Bishops, affirmed that: "whoever meets Jesus Christ meets Judaism" (*Insegnamenti*, vol. III/2, 1980, 1272).[19]

As former Prefect of the Congregation for the Doctrine of Faith, Ratzinger focuses on the theological implications of Jewish-Christian dialogue. He is acutely aware of the theological tension between the recognition of the Jewish other and the truth and unicity of the Christian faith. The question is how he would deal with some of the difficult theological questions that have emerged from Jewish-Christian dialogue — questions regarding the relation between the two covenants, the doctrinal understanding of the relationship between the Church as 'People of God' and 'God's People' Israel,"[20] the incarnation and Jesus' messiahship, the relation between the Church and the Kingdom of God, etc. These questions require an authentic and coherent theological response, and it seems that in this regard there remains quite some work to be done. What is more, there are reasons to doubt whether the pontificate of Pope Benedict XVI will display the same resolution that will allow the theology of Jewish-Christian dialogue to take new steps forward.

Though Benedict XVI time and again expresses his willingness to continue along the line of his predecessor, he does not seem to

---

[19] Address of His Holiness Pope Benedict XVI on the Occasion of His Visit to the Synagogue of Cologne, August 19, 2005 www.jcrelations.net.

[20] Eugene Fisher, "The Evolution of a Tradition: From *Nostra Aetate* to the *Notes*. International Catholic-Jewish Liaison Committee," *Fifteen Years of Catholic-Jewish Dialogue: 1970-1985* (Rome: Libreria Editrice Vaticana/Libreria Editrice Lateranense, 1988) 239.

embody the same dialogical spirit as John Paul II. He maintains what can only be described as a rather ambiguous theological position on the question of supersessionist theology. According to John Pawlikowski, President of the International Council of Christians and Jews (ICCJ), this became clear in an address given by Benedict XVI at St. Peter's Square on March 15, 2006.[21] "Launching a new cycle of catechesis on the theme of the relationship between Christ and the Church, the Pope spoke of the arrival of the definitive eschatological time in Jesus, 'the time for rebuilding God's people of the twelve tribes, which is now converted into a universal people, the Church'."[22] The Pope's theological ambiguity on supersessionism is also brought out in the contribution of Marianne Moyaert and Didier Pollefeyt in this volume. Focusing on the Pope' decision to revise the Good Friday Prayer, they show that Benedict XVI reveals traces of a supersessionist interpretation of the relation between Israel and the Church, which leads to a lack of clarity on the question whether the Church has a mission towards the Jews. This ambiguity has "given way to overt advocacy in some circles: in the pronouncements of certain prominent cardinals ... and in the growth of certain organizations for the 'ingrafting' of Jews to the Church."[23] That the question of whether the Church has a mission to the Jews is even raised and then does not receive a clear negative answer, only shows that the ecclesial climate surrounding Jewish-Catholic dialogue no longer exhibits the same dialogical openness as that of *Nostra Aetate*. What this portends for the future of Catholic-Jewish dialogue is perhaps already illustrated by the decision of the Italian Rabbis to pull out

[21] Unpublished lecture by prof. J. T. Pawlikowski at St. Paul's University, Ottawa, Canada, on October 30, 2008.

[22] Pawlikowski, *ibid.*

[23] Mary C. Boys, "Does the Catholic Church Have a Mission 'with' Jews or 'to' Jews?," *Studies in Christian Jewish Relations* 3 (2008) 1-19, 1.

of the Italian Catholic Church's annual celebration of Judaism, held on January 17, 2009.[24]

Given this perspective, it seems important not only to recall the firm belief of Pope John Paul II in the importance of Jewish-Christian dialogue. In the same spirit we therefore ask: *Can we keep the memory of Nostra Aetate alive? Can we keep faith with one another? Can we find the courage to face one another, to challenge one another? Can our relation be an 'in-between' where God may reveal Himself?* This book is inspired by *Nostra Aetate*, addressing some of the difficult theological challenges that lie ahead of us. It aims to recall John Paul II's conviction that God's covenant with Israel was "never revoked" and asks the burning question what this means for the relation of the Church to the Jewish people. It takes *Nostra Aetate* as an ongoing challenge to develop new theological reflections in the dialogical spirit of Vatican II. The contributors in this volume therefore do not only look to the past, but also critically articulate the challenges and obstacles confronting Jewish-Christian relations today, all the while looking forward to strengthening the dialogue. They not only show the resolution of naming the resistances against dialogue, the remnants of substitution theology, the asymmetry in Jewish-Christian dialogue; they set out to develop new perspectives for the theology of Jewish-Christian dialogue.

In the introductory chapter, Mathijs Lamberigts and Leo Declerck (Faculty of Theology, Katholieke Universiteit Leuven, Belgium) sketch the historical development of the declaration on 'the relationship of the Church to non-Christian religions', with special attention to the way *Nostra Aetate* deals with Judaism. They first draw attention to three individuals, without whom the Second Vatican Council would probably not have addressed the matter of the

---

[24] *Italy's Jews: Pope Benedict Negating 50 Years of Interfaith Progress*, January 13, 2009; http://www.haaretz.com/.

Church's relations to the Jews: Pope John XXIII, Cardinal Augustine Bea and Jules Isaac. Lamberigts and Declerck then sketch the
preparatory phase in which the *Secretariatus ad christianorum unitatem fovendam* formulated the schema, which would ultimately
become *Nostra Aetate* 4, namely "the establishment of a position
on anti-Semitism and a reflection on the part of the Church on its
own Jewish roots."[25] Following this, they reconstruct in detail the
many conciliar (inter)sessions during the council that led up to promulgation of the document. In doing so, they not only highlight
the delicacy of the issue in light of the political situation in the
Middle East at that moment, they also show how the declaration on
the Jews (*Nostra Aetate* 4) "made it clear that the Roman Catholic
church was ultimately capable of setting aside ancient tradition
where sound biblical, historical and cultural arguments insisted
upon it."[26]

Moving beyond the historical perspective John Pawlikowski
(Catholic Theological Union, Chicago, USA) examines developments in the Church's thinking on the key issues of covenant and
mission. He surveys recent trends in biblical scholarship, the ideas
of theologians connected to Christian-Jewish dialogue such as Johann
Baptist Metz, and Church leaders like Cardinal Walter Kasper and
Cardinal Joseph Ratzinger (now Pope Benedict XVI). Pawlikowski
tries to develop a theological model for the Christian-Jewish relationship that both safeguards Christological newness while at the
same time creating authentic theological space for Judaism.

David Meyer (Rabbi of the Brighton and Hove New Synagogue, United Kingdom) praises the courage it took forty years
ago for the Church to completely rethink its relationship with

---

[25] Lamberigts and Declerck, "Vatican II on the Jews: A Historical Survey,"
in this volume, 55.
[26] *Ibid.*, 23.

other religions and with Judaism in particular. With equal courage he goes on to address some of the real (theological) difficulties for Jewish-Christian dialogue. Reading *Nostra Aetate* as a Jew, he admits to be shocked at times by the way this dialogical document speaks about the Jewish people in its relation to the Church. If we want to move ahead in the dialogue, he argues, Christians need to learn to listen in earnest to the Jewish other.

Simon Schoon (Theologische Universiteit Kampen, The Netherlands) reflects on the concept, 'People of God'. During Vatican II, the Roman Catholic Church re-discovered the Church as 'the People of God on the way'. The question then is: does a renewal of the relationship between Christians and Jews in the 21th century demand the radical theological step to give up the title 'People of God' for the Church? Schoon chooses to speak of Israel as the 'first-chosen People of God' and of the Church as the 'also-chosen ecumenical People of God from all the nations'.[27] He proposes to view the 'rootedness of the Church in (the People of) Israel' as one of the *notae ecclesiae*. In the Protestant view, the Church is the 'People of God' and holy when it is a Church of *metanoia*, of repentance, because the Church must be *semper reformanda*, 'always reforming'. Thus, he states: "After a long and dreadful history, the church and the Jewish people could perhaps, on their different ways to the kingdom of God join forces in a competition for holiness to work for the restoration of the world, separately and together."[28]

In her contribution, Mary C. Boys (Union Theological Seminary, New York, USA) confirms that *Nostra Aetate* intended to overcome

---

[27] Simon Schoon, "'The New People of God': A Protestant View," in this volume, 93-116, 112.

[28] *Ibid.*, 114.

supersessionist theology, thereby bringing about a transformation in the relation between Israel and the Church. However, the question remains: what happens *after supersessionism*? It is one thing to affirm that Israel remains God's beloved people, it is quite another thing to formulate a consistent theology of Jewish-Christian relations. If Jews are still covenanted with God and not, as was taught for centuries, unfaithful and blind, then what, if anything, can or should we say about their salvation? Does their covenanted life with God in any way involves Jesus Christ? Boys rightly points out that these and other questions, mainly concerning soteriology, demand serious theological reflection. Indeed, the dialogue which commenced after *Nostra Aetate* raises many questions, even unsettling ones. However, Boys remains convinced that it is in and through dialogue with Israel, that theology is enlivened.

Marianne Moyaert and Didier Pollefeyt (Katholieke Universiteit Leuven, Belgium) focus on the post-conciliar developments within the Catholic theology of Jewish-Christian relations. For them one of the most urgent questions is whether Catholic theology has actually succeeded in overcoming supersessionism. In this perspective they turn to the work of Joseph Ratzinger, now Pope Benedict XVI, who can be regarded as representative of Catholic teaching on Jewish-Christian relations. Their analysis of Ratzinger's thinking shows that Catholic theology still wrestles with supersessionist ideas and has still not succeeded in developing a coherent and authentic theology of Jewish-Christian relations. Moreover, Moyaert and Pollefeyt highlight the negative consequences of this theological lacuna on the dialogue between Israel and the Church. Forty years after *Nostra Aetate* there still remains much work to be done.

Marianne MOYAERT & Didier POLLEFEYT

VATICAN II ON THE JEWS
A HISTORICAL SURVEY

Mathijs LAMBERIGTS & Leo DECLERCK

By way of introduction, it is important to note that the very fact that the Second Vatican Council addressed the matter of the Church's relations with the Jews in one of its documents, *Nostra Aetate*, is due in large measure to two individuals: Pope John XXIII and Cardinal Augustine Bea.[1] It would seem appropriate at this juncture to take a brief look at the beginning of the pontificate of John XXIII, a moment characterized by a series of symbolic deeds. John XXIII insisted from the outset that he planned to exercise his responsibility as bishop of Rome. As a result, he took possession of the cathedral of Saint John Lateran with great solemnity and set out to visit hospitals and prisons in the city. Familiar as he was with the tragedy of the Jews — John XXIII was actively involved in endeavors to save Jews from deportation and inevitable death in the concentration camps[2] — he was to ensure that the term *perfidi* be scrapped for the first time from the prayer for the Jews during the

---

[1] The literature on Vatican II and the Jews is abundant; see, for example, Arthur Gilbert, *The Vatican Council and the Jews* (Cleveland, OH/New York: World Publishing Co., 1968). With respect to the Catholic teaching on non-Christian religions during the Council see, for example, Miika Ruokanen, *The Catholic Doctrine of Non-Christian Religions according to the Second Vatican Council*, Studies in Christian Mission, 7 (Leiden/New York/Cologne: Brill, 1992).

[2] Cf. in this regard Alberto Melloni, *Fra Istanbul, Atene e la guerra: La missione di A. G. Roncalli (1935-1944)*, Testi e ricerche di scienze religiose, Nuova Serie, 10 (Genova: Marietti, 1992) 258-279.

intercessions on Good Friday of 1959.[3] It was to come as no surprise, therefore, that the Jews invited him in 1960 to intervene against a revival of anti-Semitism current at the time and particularly evident at the opening of a new synagogue in Cologne in the same year.[4]

Brief reference should also be made to Cardinal Augustine Bea (1881-1968) who, as president of the newly established Secretariat for the Promotion of Christian Unity (*Secretariatus ad christianorum unitatem fovendam*, henceforth SCUF), became John XXIII's trusted representative in matters related to ecumenism. Although the question of Christian unity was a thorny one in Roman circles, the pope explicitly desired that Vatican II be an ecumenical council.[5] Bea represented living proof that age had nothing to do with a person's progressive or conservative point of view. At 79 years of age, he took the helm at the SCUF. It was partly under his influence that the Council was to finally follow an ecumenical trajectory. The fact that he was granted the Peace Prize of the German bookshops in 1996 together with the Protestant Visser 't Hooft of the World Council of Churches is far from accidental.[6] As a German, Bea was to play an important and constructive role in the genesis and evolution of a document on the Jews that was ultimately to give rise to *Nostra Aetate # 4*.

---

[3] Cf. Giovanni XXIII [Angelo Roncalli], *Lettere ai familiari 1901-1962*, 2, ed. Loris Francesco Capovilla (Rome, 1968) 484. The fact that John XXIII was opposed to derogatory and prejudiced statements concerning pagans, Jews, Muslims etc. is also evident in *AAS* 51 (1959) 595.

[4] Cf. Gilbert, *The Vatican Council*, appendix G.

[5] See in this regard Giuseppe Alberigo, "The Announcement of the Council: From the Security of the Fortress to the Lure of the Quest," *History of Vatican II*, ed. Giuseppe Alberigo and Joseph A. Komonchak (New York/Leuven: Maryknoll, NY/Peeters, 1995-2006) 1: 28-30.

[6] For further information on the life of Cardinal Bea see the lively biography written by Stjepan Schmidt, *Augustin Bea, Der Kardinal Der Einheit* (Graz: Styria, 1989).

Less well known perhaps, at least with respect to the prehistory of *Nostra Aetate* # 4, is the fact that the Jew Jules Isaac[7] was involved at the time in significant efforts to promote contact between Christians and Jews.[8] In his work *Jésus et Israël*, published in 1948, he demonstrated how Christianity bore responsibility for a flawed representation of the Jews and their religion on account of the manner with which it presented them. The work was not intended as an attack on Christianity as such, but rather on the way in which Christians had offered a distorted image of the Jews at certain moments in time. The fact that Isaac did not wish to set himself up as an opponent of Christianity is evident from the group *Amitié judéo-chrétienne*, which he established in the same year with a view to improving the exchange of information between both religions. Of primary importance for the increased attention being paid to Jewish-Christian relations was the meeting between Isaac and John XXIII in 1960, an encounter that inspired Isaac to continue his endeavors, encouraged by the fact that he had found in the pope an open ear and a man who had demonstrated himself as a protector of the Jews during World War II. As a matter of fact, the pope acceded to Isaac's request to raise the question of the Jews during the coming Council,[9] putting him in contact with Cardinal Bea to concretize matters.[10]

[7] With respect to relations between Jews and French Catholics see Pierre Pierrard, *Juifs et catholiques français: De Drumont à Jules Isaac (1886-1945)*, Cerf-histoire (Paris: Cerf, 1970).

[8] Jules Isaac was born in Rennes in France in 1877. During World War II, the historian lost his wife and daughter. Both were arrested by the Nazis and died in Auschwitz. Isaac himself died in 1963.

[9] Cf. in this regard Jules Isaac, *The Teaching of Contempt: Christian Roots of Anti-Semitism* (New York: Holt, 1964) 14.

[10] Cf. Michael Phayer, *The Catholic Church and the Holocaust (1930-1965)* (Bloomington, IN: Indiana University Press, 2000) 208.

THE PREPARATORY PHASE

In the course of the Council's preparatory phase, the question of relations with the Jews was treated in particular by the SCUF.[11] During an explanatory statement given by Cardinal Bea at a meeting of the SCUF in November 1960, it became apparent that the Secretariat considered relations with the Jews together with the relationship between the two Testaments as one of its primary tasks.[12] It was the initial intention that the SCUF would prepare material to be presented to the various preparatory commissions. Given the lack of ecumenical openness in some of the preparatory commissions — in particular the theological commission —, however, the SCUF gradually began to compose its own texts with a view to the forthcoming Council. The question of the Jews was entrusted to sub-commission 10, in which Gregory Baum and John Oesterreicher, both converts from Judaism, were to play an important role. Oesterreicher in particular was responsible for an influential text in which he called upon the Church to recognize its Jewish roots, defy the idea that the Jews were the subject of a divine curse, and proclaim that reconciliation between Jews and Christians was an element of the Church's eschatological expectation. He concluded with a call for the condemnation of anti-Semitism.[13] While the text in question was well received in discussions held in April 1961, by August of the same year it had already become clear that the presentation and approval of a positive text on relations with the Jews was far from evident. Indeed, objections were

---

[11] Giovanni Miccoli, "Two Sensitive Issues: Religious Freedom and the Jews," *History of Vatican II*, 5: 137.

[12] Cf. Komonchak, "The Struggle for the Council during the Preparation of Vatican II (1960-1962)," *History of Vatican II*, 1: 265.

[13] *Ibid.*, 1: 270.

expected form the Arabic world in this regard. Furthermore, within the world of Catholic theologians and bishops, not everyone was sufficiently prepared to look at Judaism in a positive manner. Concerns were expressed during the November 1961 meeting that a statement from the approaching Council on the complex political problems of the Middle East might give rise to difficulties, especially in light of the fact that such a statement would ultimately be based on a particular interpretation of the Scriptures. A short text was finally put together which was ultimately left untreated during the meeting of the central preparatory commission of June 1962 because of a concern not to intervene in the bitter discussions that were raging between the Jews and the Arabs. Every effort was being made to avoid the impression that the Catholic Church had opted politically for one side or the other or that it was prepared to recognize the State of Israel.[14] It should be stated from the outset, however, that given the hostile situation in the Middle East, any statement from the leadership of the Church could be effortlessly explained by either side of the conflict as support for or criticism of its own ambitions. The text was thus left untreated for primarily political reasons.[15] In passing it should be mentioned that only on October 19th, 1962 the SCUF was granted equal status to the other conciliar commissions.

It should be noted in passing that the announcement of the approaching Council elicited little if any reaction within Jewish circles. This is hardly surprising since the stated goal of the Council

[14] *Acta et Documenta Concilio Oecumenico Vaticano II Apparando (Series II: praeparatoria)*, 4: 22-23. Cf. also Komonchak, "The Struggle," 271 (with additional literature).

[15] It should be noted at the same time, however, that the presence of a Catholic minority within the population of Palestine also made it difficult for the Holy See to recognize the State of Israel.

was internal renewal and the establishment of a constructive Catholic dialogue with other Christian churches.[16]

THE FIRST SESSION AND THE FIRST INTERSESSION

The declaration on relations with the Jews did not find its way onto the agenda of the first session of the Council, although occasional reference was made thereto in the context of other debates, including the discussion of the schema *De Ecclesia*.[17] At the same time, however, the SCUF continued to insist that a document on the Jews deserved a place in the conciliar program.[18] This was also the desire of John XXIII himself, as is apparent from his reaction on December 13th 1962 to a memorandum written by Cardinal Bea, in which the latter had suggested that Catholic preaching concerning the Jews in the past had not always lived up to the standards of the Christian command to love one's neighbor. The pope agreed to reinstate the schema concerning the Jews as part of the conciliar program.[19] In the meantime, it had gradually become known that a text concerning the Jews had existed in the preparatory phase. Indeed, various Jewish communities, including that of Strasbourg, were of the opinion that the Council, the first since Auschwitz,

[16] Cf. Jose Oscar Beozzo, "The External Climate," *History of Vatican II*, 1: 392-393.

[17] Cf. the intervention of the Mexican bishop Mendez Arceo, in *Acta Synodalia Sacrosancti Concilii Oecumenici Vaticani II* [henceforth: *AS*] I/4, 340-341.

[18] See Mauro Velati, *Una difficile transizione: Il cattolicesimo tra unionismo ed ecumenismo*, Testi e ricerche di scienze religiose, Nuova serie, 16 (Bologna: Il Mulino, 1996) 380-381.

[19] See in this regard, for example, Georges Cottier, "L'historique de la déclaration," *Les relations de l'Église avec les religions non chrétiennes. Déclaration "Nostra Aetate": Texte latin et traduction française*, ed. Antonin Marcel Henry; Unam sanctam, 61 (Paris: Cerf, 1966) 40.

could not allow itself to pass without making a statement on the Jews.[20]

Germany was also positively inclined towards a text on the Jews. To this end, Cardinal Döpfner (Munich) dispatched a letter on May 27th 1963 to Cardinal Cicognani in which he lamented the fact that the decree concerning the Jews had not been included in the *Elenchus* of the schemata proposed for discussion, although this had been suggested earlier in the central commission and was the wish of many of the conciliar fathers.[21] The letter went on to explicitly request the inclusion of the subject in the list of schemata proposed for discussion. Döpfner motivated his request by pointing out that everyone was now aware that a text had been put together and that the abandonment thereof at this stage would cause considerable surprise and occasion potential speculation, especially since many already had their doubts concerning the relationship between the Roman Catholic Church and the Jews. Furthermore, should the Council consider it necessary to speak about the relationship between Catholic and non-Catholic Christians, then a document on the Jews would certainly be appropriate.[22]

Efforts undertaken in the meantime to integrate the decree on the Jews into the schema *De Oecumenismo* encountered resistance for both political and ecclesiastical reasons: both the Arab nations and the churches in the Middle East considered it inappropriate. Problems with respect to the said schema, however, were not restricted to the aforementioned resistance. The text employed the term "church" when it spoke of Orthodox churches while it used the term "communities" with respect to Protestants. Furthermore,

---

[20] Yves Congar, *Mon Journal du Concile*, 1. Présenté et annoté par Éric Mahieu. Avant-propos de Dominique Congar. Préface de Bernard Dupuy (Paris: Cerf, 2002) 357.

[21] *AS* VI/2, 182-183.

[22] *Ibid.*

the inclusion of the Jews in the same schema as that dealing with non-Catholic Christian denominations might have given the impression that everything non-Catholic had been lumped together under one and the same category.[23] It should be noted, nevertheless, that Protestant circles experienced the explicit reference to the bond with the Jews as an important element for ecumenism.[24] The segment on the Jews was ultimately to find its place in the schema *De Oecumenismo* during this phase of the Council.

THE SECOND SESSION

On November 8th 1963, a text was distributed entitled *De catholicorum habitudine ad non christianos et maxime ad Iudaeos*, constituting chapter 4 of the Schema *De Oecumenismo*.[25] The text was fairly short. The introduction explained why it was necessary to make a statement concerning dialogue and cooperation with non-Christians: they also worship God and strive to live an ethical life. Judaism enjoyed a unique place among the non-Christian religions. Indeed, the Church recognized that the roots of its faith and election were already present among the patriarchs and the prophets.

[23] Cf. Joseph Famerée, "Bishops and Dioceses and the Communications Media (November 5-25, 1963)," *History of Vatican II*, 3: 164.

[24] Famerée, "Bishops and Dioceses," 164.

[25] For the text see *AS* II/5, 431-432. The fact that Jewish circles were also looking forward with interest to such a text is apparent from a telegram addressed to Cardinal Suenens on October 24th 1963 by P. Philippson, president of the Central Israelite Consistory of Belgium in which the latter expressed his hope that the Council would establish its position on the relationship between Catholics and Jews in such a way that the discrimination suffered by Jews in the past would thus be brought to an end; cf. Leo Declerck and Eddy Louchez, *Inventaire des Papiers conciliaires du cardinal L.-J. Suenens*, Cahiers de la Revue théologique de Louvain, 31 (Louvain-la-Neuve: Faculté de Théologie, 1998), nr. 1618.

All Christians are likewise children of Abraham according to their faith (Gal 3:7). In spite of the fact that the Jews remain far from Christ, it would be unjust to describe them as a people cursed by God or as murderers of God. It would be wrong to argue that all the Jews of Jesus' day or of the present should be held responsible for the death of Jesus. Priests were asked to say nothing in the context of preaching or catechesis that might initiate or encourage hatred and contempt towards the Jews. Moreover, Jesus, Mary and the apostles were themselves Jews. For precisely this reason, the Council wished to encourage and recommend an exchange of information and respect to be acquired via study and dialogue. The Council condemned everything that might lead to the hatred and persecution of the Jews, in the past as well as the present.

While the text in question was not discussed during the second session, frequent reference was made thereto within the context of the discussion of the first three chapters of the schema *De oecumenismo* (18th to 21st November 1963). It should be noted with respect to the schema concerning the Jews that the text limited itself to a strictly religious standpoint. In his presentation of the general report, Cardinal Cicognani, Secretary of State and president of the Commission for the Eastern Churches, pointed to the fact that love of the Scriptures united Jews and Christians. Given the fact that the message of Christ was also explicitly addressed to the Jews, the Church did not exclude the Jews from its own spiritual mission. In his presentation of the fourth chapter of the schema on November 19th 1963,[26] Cardinal Bea, the primary driving force behind this declaration concerning the Jews, explicitly repeated that the matter had been approached from a purely religious perspective and that the text had no intention whatsoever to interfere in matters related to the relationship between the Arab nations and the State

---

[26] Cf. his detailed report in *AS* II/5, 481-485.

of Israel. The decree concerning the Jews was addressed to Catholics with a view to indicating the attitude they, as followers of Christ, ought to show towards the Jews. In his introduction, Cardinal Bea first made reference to the reason why the text had not been discussed in the central commission in June 1962. The text that lay before the Council was intended as a positive statement concerning the gift that the Church of Christ had received from the chosen people of Israel, namely the Old Testament. The Cardinal also underlined the fact that the Church was the continuation of the people of Israel. The necessity of a text concerning the Jews, according to Bea, also had to do with the fact of anti-Semitism that had evolved throughout the centuries to reach its climax in German National Socialism, which had aimed at the annihilation of the Jewish people. The Cardinal argued with vigor that such an annihilation was unable to claim any support from ecclesial teaching. Bea was particularly clear on the claim that the Jews had been responsible for the death of Christ: the Jewish people of today were not to be held responsible for the death of Christ. Indeed the same was valid for the majority of Jews in Jesus' days: they had not cooperated with their leaders with regard to Jesus' condemnation. The accusation of deicide ought thus to be explicitly rejected.

It ought to be noted at this juncture that, from the Roman Catholic perspective, a text on the Jews was a somewhat delicate matter, especially given the attitude of Pius XII to the Jews during World War II. While Paul VI vehemently defended his predecessor in this question, Pius XII's silence with respect to the Jews during the war gave rise to significant criticism from elsewhere.[27]

---

[27] Reference can be made in this regard to the play *Der Stellvertreter* by Rolf Hochhuth, which struck an enormously negative note — especially in Italy — on account of its biting condemnation of the Vatican's attitude towards the Jews during World War II. See also Miccoli, "Two Sensitive Issues," 140.

As noted above, the schema as such was not discussed in its entirety during the second session of the Council. In their interventions with respect to other chapters of the schema, however, the bishops of the Middle East made it clear that they considered it inopportune to make a statement about the other Christian churches and even less appropriate to enter into discussion concerning non-Christian religions. The said bishops were afraid, moreover, that any such discussion of non-Christian religions might give rise to problems for Christians in regions in which they constituted a minority.[28] Others were of the opinion that if anything was to be said about the Jews then it should be said in relation to the other world religions.[29] Among those who introduced such observations, some were positively inclined towards a text on the Jews while arguing in favor of broadening the perspective to include other religions. Where the bishops of the Middle East naturally wished to include Islam in the discussion, bishops from the Far East, such as Cardinal Doi of Tokyo, likewise insisted that Buddhism and Confucianism should not be ignored. Indeed, the same could also be said with respect to Animism (Africa) and Hinduism (Asia). Cardinal Doi was of the opinion that the Church ought to explicitly recognize that these world religions also exhibited traces of the truth and that this fact could serve as the basis upon which the said religions might be sensitized to the preaching of the gospel. It went without saying that the Church ought to express its respect for the other world religions and take cooperation with all people of good will as its point of departure and guiding motivation.

---

[28] See in this regard the interventions of Cardinal Tappouni, Patriarch Sidarouss, and Patriarch Maximos IV Saigh (AS II/5, 527-528; 541-542; 542-544).

[29] Thus, for example, Cardinal Ruffini (Palermo), Msgr. Gori (Jerusalem), Msgr. Jelmini (Apostolic Administrator of Lugano) speaking on behalf of the bishops of Switzerland (AS II/5, 528-530; 557; 600-602); cf. also Congar, *Mon Journal du Concile*, 1: 544.

It is sometimes forgotten that some theologians and Council fathers who were positive towards the Jews and Judaism did not consider an independent text on the Jews to be necessary, arguing that it was possible to speak about them in the schema concerning the Church — in particular in the chapter entitled *De populo Dei* — or in the schema on the Church in the Modern World in which reference could be made in the context of the condemnation of every form of discrimination.[30] An additional element that ought to be noted here is the fact that a number of individuals were not positively inclined towards the Jews and for a variety of reasons, all of which shared the same common root: Christians ultimately had good reason to be against the Jews.[31]

Some speakers, moreover, strongly favored a text on the Jews, but preferred to see it cast in an independent document.[32] While opinions clearly varied, a significant group of participants nevertheless lamented the fact that there had been no discussion of chapters IV and V (on religious freedom) of the schema *De Oecumenismo*. Given the additional fact that neither chapter had been subject to a vote, it remained unclear whether it was acceptable to proceed on the basis of the texts at hand and, if so, under what conditions. At the same time, the Council fathers were given the opportunity to submit their observations in writing on precisely these two chapters.

Several reasons have been given to explain why the text was not discussed during the second session. We limit ourselves here to a

[30] Miccoli, "Two Sensitive Issues," 141; cf. also Congar, *Mon Journal du Concile*, 2: 25.

[31] *Ibid.*

[32] Thus Cardinal Léger (Montreal), Patriarch Batanian (Armenian Patriarch, Lebanon) (*AS* II/5, 550-552; 558-560). The fact that such a debate represented more or less every possible opinion is apparent from the intervention of Cardinal Meyer (Chicago), who was of the opinion that chapters IV and V ought to remain as they were in the section on ecumenism; *AS* II/5, 597.

brief summary: the pope's forthcoming trip to the Holy Land might have been placed in danger; protest stemming from the Arab nations and addressed to the Secretary of State via their diplomats had left a strong impression; the theological critique expressed by the minority had been taken seriously. While opinions evidently varied once again, uncertainty with respect to our text continued to predominate at the end of the second session.

The Second Intersession

During the second intersession, the Secretariat for Christian Unity was to hold its plenary meeting from February 24th to March 7th 1964. The Coordinating Commission had granted the SCUF the necessary freedom. It was at liberty to decide for itself whether the text should be preserved within the context of the schema on ecumenism or be cast rather in an independent declaration.[33] The SCUF decided to maintain the text on the Jews as it was, given its objective importance and in light of the attention the matter had

---

[33] This would appear to be the suggestion found in the report of Cardinal Döpfner (*AS* V/2, 89), which already considers the possibility of framing the statement on the Jews within a broader declaration on the Jews, the other non-Christian religions and all people of good will. The official minutes (*AS* V/2, 95), on the other hand, leave the impression that the decision had been made to integrate the segment on the Jews into the document on the Church in the Modern World, but this does not square with action ultimately taken by the SCUF. We know from a letter addressed by Cardinal Bea to Msgr. Felici and dated January 14th 1964, that according to Bea the possibility was being considered of inserting a paragraph on the monotheistic religions in general and Islam in particular into the segment on the Jews. It would appear that Bea had an appendix to the schema on ecumenism in mind in this regard; cf. *AS* V/2, 104. The official minutes of the Coordinating Commission of January 15th make it clear that the right of initiative at that moment was given into the hands of the SCUF; *AS* V/2, 120.

generated among the fathers (their written observations were nothing less than voluminous!). At the same time, however, it was also decided to relocate the text to a sort of appendix to the schema on ecumenism.[34]

The SCUF's text was discussed by the Coordinating Commission on April 16th and 17th 1964. It was suggested that the text on the Jews ought to be placed within the broader framework of a statement on monotheistic religions, whereby the matter could be considered in more general terms by emphasizing the importance of universal fraternity, for example, and by condemning every form of racial or national oppression.[35] The Coordinating Commission desired to account for the objections stemming from the Arabic world[36] and exhibit sensitivity with respect to the fears of Christians in the Middle East. Furthermore, the fact that the text might be read by some as an acquittal of the Jews with regard to the accusation of deicide represented a source of difficulty. Cicognani was also of the opinion that it would be better to rework the text and add a statement concerning the Muslims and the other religions.[37] All this was to result in a proposed declaration on the Jews and the non-Christian religions based on the following criteria: shared source;

---

[34] This procedure had already been suggested by Bea and had been proposed during the plenary meeting of the SCUF (February 24th – March 7th); cf. AS V/2, 168. The final decision was supported by an overwhelming majority of the members of the SCUF (19 to 1); cf. AS V/2, 152. The SCUF exhibited a degree of caution with respect to Islam, arguing that the theme in question was beyond its competence.

[35] Cf. AS V/2, 292.

[36] Rumors abounded at the time that the Arabic world was threatening to sever diplomatic relations with the Vatican if the text on the Jews was allowed to remain in the schema on ecumenism; see Congar, *Mon Journal du Concile*, 2: 59-60.

[37] AS V/2, 285ff. Cicognani was not only chair of the Coordinating Commission but also Secretary of State and as such he was highly sensitive towards potentially negative reactions from within the diplomatic world.

other non-Christians are also children of God; emphasis on universal fraternity; rejection of every form of oppression of peoples and races.[38] It became evident that in light of this option, relations with the Jews were to be considered in a completely different context than had hitherto been the case, although the various versions of the text that were to follow maintained a clear degree of consistency in terms of content. Indeed, reference was no longer made to the Jews within an ecumenical framework, but rather within the framework of relations with the world religions — in particular with Islam — and within the framework of universal fraternity.[39] It is worthy of note at this juncture that the passage relating to deicide in the new draft text was to be significantly moderated.[40]

The Coordinating Commission's recommendations were quickly implemented.[41] As early as May 6th, Bea was ready to submit the *Adnexum* via Felici to the pope.[42] The text was divided into three subsections: part one dealing with the heritage shared by both Christians and Jews, part two reflecting on the fact that all human beings share the same God as their father, and part three condemning every form of discrimination.[43] Globally speaking, the text enjoyed the approval of Paul VI.[44] It was submitted to the Coordinating Commission where it was accepted on June 26th 1964.

---

[38] *AS* V/2, 292.

[39] *AS* V/2, 572.

[40] Cf. the letter addressed by Cicognani to Bea, dated April 18th 1964; see also Miccoli, "Two Sensitive Issues," 145.

[41] On the role of Congar see his *Mon Journal du Concile*, 2: 70-72, 82.

[42] *AS* VI/3, 159.

[43] *AS* VI/3, 160-161.

[44] *AS* VI/3, 180. The pope closely followed developments with regard to the text and sought to present the question of the Jews in the best possible light; cf. *AS* V/2, 548-549; for additional evidence of the pope's interest see *AS* V/2, 572-573. The fact that the pope kept a close eye on the matter is evident from a letter

In order to make it clear that the Jews of today and the great majority of the Jews of Jesus' day should not be held responsible for Christ's death, a statement was added upon the suggestion of Cardinal Lercaro that Christ died for the sins of all humanity.[45] During the discussion, Felici complained about the fact that in light of a number of letters received from the United States, it had become clear that elements of the content of the text had been leaked.[46]

In addition to the usual work of the Council, public opinion was also managed via articles and speeches by Cardinal Bea, for example, or by Msgr. Heenan, Archbishop of Westminster. The lengthy declaration of the Arab League at the United Nations was also of great significance. It stated that both the nations that belonged to the league and the Christians living within them looked forward with joy to welcoming a text that would deal exclusively with the religious aspect of Judaism. The text explicitly stated that the members of the League were well aware of the profound connections that existed between Islam and the Jewish religion.

A number of important decisions made by Paul VI were also to give strong support to a more positive attitude with respect to a declaration concerning the Jews and the other non-Christian religions. Reference should be made in the first instance to the pope's visit to the Holy Land, a visit announced at the closure of the second session on December 4th 1963. In addition, the pope's decision to set up a new secretariat for non-Christian religions also had a positive and influential role to play in the matter,[47] as did the publication of the encyclical *Ecclesiam suam*.

addressed by Msgr. Felici to Cardinal Bea, dated June 1st 1964; cf. *AS* V/2, 525-526.

[45] Cf. *AS* V/2, 639, 654-655.

[46] *AS* V/2, 639.

[47] *AS* VI/3, 181-183. Relations with the Jews continued to fall under the auspices of the SCUF.

While we are well aware that the pope's visit to the Holy Land was intended in the first instance to have an ecumenical goal, the trip nevertheless also provided the pope with the opportunity to meet with non-Christians.[48] In his address to the Israeli president Zalman Shazar and that to king Hussein of Jordan, the pope underlined the spiritual character of his visit and the fact that he saw himself as a pilgrim of peace.[49] In a speech delivered in Bethlehem on December 6th, the pope explicitly addressed himself to all the adherents of monotheism. In the course of the second intersession, the pope was to return with regularity to his visit to the Middle East, drawing attention to the valued aspects of the aforementioned monotheistic faiths.

On May 17th 1964, the Feast of Pentecost, the pope announced the establishment of the Secretariat for Non-Christian Religions, with Cardinal Marella as its first chair.[50]

The fact that Paul VI was a firm supporter of dialogue is also evident from his first encyclical, *Ecclesiam suam*, published on August 6th 1964. The encyclical made explicit reference to the monotheistic faiths, *in casu* Judaism and Islam. In spite of the great respect these and other Afro-Asian religions deserved, however, the pope nevertheless insisted that Christianity was the only true religion, expressing his hope that the latter would ultimately be recognized by all those who seek and worship God. Such a conviction, the

---

[48] The visit elicited both praise and criticism. See in this regard Jean Marie Delmaire, "Une ouverture prudente: Paul VI, le judaïsme et Israël," *Paul VI et la modernité dans l'Église: Actes du colloque organisé par l'École française de Rome (Rome 2-4 juin 1983)*, Collection de l'École française de Rome, 72 (Rome: École française de Rome, 1984) 821-835, esp. p. 821.

[49] Cf. Delmaire, "Une ouverture prudente," 828.

[50] Secretary of State Cicognani already makes reference to this in a letter addressed to Msgr. Felici, dated March 14th 1964; cf. *AS* VI/3, 99, in which Marella's name is explicitly mentioned.

pope insisted, need not imply that Christians were blind to the spiritual and moral values inherent in other religions. On the contrary, Christians desired to join with other faiths in defending and promoting those values that support religious freedom, human fraternity, reputable culture, social well-being and public order. Dialogue and cooperation was thus possible at all these levels.[51]

The papal initiatives outlined above must also be interpreted in light of the disappointment expressed, for example, by a number of American bishops. Direct reference can be made in this regard to a letter addressed to the pope by Cardinal Joseph Ritter of Saint Louis on March 12th 1964: "The enormous out-pouring of good will which greeted the First Session of the Council has been greatly tempered by the failure of the Second Session to treat of or even to accept as a basis for discussion the proposed drafts on The Jews and on Religious Liberty. Although these two chapters are certainly not the only topics which ought to be treated by the Council, they are universally interpreted as indications of the Church's willingness or refusal to concern itself with the problems of our age."[52] When rumors began to spread that the Coordinating Commission had interfered with the text produced by the SCUF and that the term deicide had been left out, reactions abounded from both Jewish and Catholic quarters. Catholics feared that they would lose the credibility that had been built up with the Jews,[53] while the Jews explicitly requested a return to the text of November 1963.[54]

---

[51] The fact that the encyclical did not always elicit a positive reception is evident, for example, in Congar, *Mon Journal du Concile*, 2: 121.

[52] See *AS* VI/3, 108.

[53] Cf. in this regard the letter of Cardinal Spellman (New York) to Cicognani, dated June 13th 1964; *AS* V/2, 543-544.

[54] See *AS* VI/3, 199 (letter of L. Rudloff OSB, abbot of Dormition Abbey, Jerusalem, dated May 10th 1964); *AS* VI/3, 200 (letter of Msgr. Helmsing, bishop of Kansas City, dated June 15th 1964); *AS* VI/3, 279 (note written by Cicognani concerning the opinion of S. E. Goldberg, member of the US Supreme Court, who

In the meantime, a number of Middle Eastern patriarchs let their voices be heard. Maximos IV Saigh, patriarch of the Melkites, wrote a letter in the name of the Melkite bishops who had been gathered in assembly from August 17th to 22nd, in which he asked for the text on the Jews to be removed from the agenda. The document, he maintained, was inopportune and unnecessary: enough had been said with respect to the relationship between the Old and New Testaments in *De Ecclesia*, and a statement on the question of racial hatred would be better placed in the schema on the Church in the Modern World.[55] Having already arrived in Rome, the Coptic Patriarch Sidarouss likewise wrote a letter in which he pointed out that the text concerning the Jews had already been abused for political and religious reasons and that the text itself was a disaster when it came to relations with other Christians (namely the Greek Orthodox) and with Islam. He concluded by noting that his own small community was already being confronted with considerable problems.[56]

Third Session

During the third session of the Council, the text on the Jews was discussed for the first time at the general assemblies of September

would appear to have spoken in the name of the major Jewish organizations and centra, dated August 28th 1964). Cf. also Congar, *Mon Journal du Concile*, 2: 119-120.

[55] *AS* VI/3, 400 (letter from Maximos to Paul VI, dated September 3rd 1964).

[56] *AS* VI/3, 401 (letter from Sidarouss to Paul VI, dated September 22nd 1964); for other reactions see *AS* VI/3, 437; 460-461; 470-471; 475. The reactions in question stem from diplomats of the Holy See, including those in Cairo, Jordan and Lebanon. In the latter instance, the reaction is clearly coming from Islamic people.

28th, 29th and 30th.[57] As is evident from the enumeration of the articles, the text continued to exist as an appendix to the schema on
ecumenism. By maintaining a connection with the latter, it became
clear that the Jewish people enjoyed a privileged relationship with
the Church on account of their shared source, namely the Old Testament. The text as it stood had acquired the status of a Declaration. The new text[58] was significantly longer that the text of 1963.
A passage had been added, for example, in which it was stated that
the unification of the Jewish people with the Church was a Christian hope. It was also stated that the God of the Old Testament and
the God of the New were one and the same and that it was not possible to pray to God if one excluded the Jews. This clearly reinforced the association between love of God and love of one's fellow human beings. Quotations from the Bible were used in
abundance. Exclusion or persecution for reasons of origin, color,
condition or culture was to be rejected. Humanity had much in
common in spite of its great diversity.

---

[57] The idea that the Council planned to speak in a positive manner with respect
to the Jews caused a degree of consternation and resistance in certain circles, as
is evident from the pamphlet that was distributed among the conciliar fathers entitled *L'Action Judéo-Maçonnique dans le Concile: Lecture exclusivement réservée
à leurs révérendissimes Pères Conciliaires*. For the text itself see Centre Lumen
Gentium (UCL), Prignon Papers, nr. 986 [An inventory was published by Joseph
Famerée, *Concile Vatican II et Église contemporaine*, 2. *Inventaire des fonds
A. Prignon et H. Wagnon*, Cahiers de la Revue théologique de Louvain, 24
(Louvain-la-Neuve: Faculté de Théologie, 1991)]. The pamphlet contained the
following statement: "Ce sont, Seigneur, les juifs faussement convertis, qui, une
fois de plus, essaient de détruire ton œuvre divine!" The text — or better *the dia-
tribe* — was primarily aimed at converts such as Oesterreicher and Baum
(cf. p. 16). Cardinal Bea himself was not spared: "Ces thèses, élaborées cer-
tainement par quelque grand rabbin, furent présentées officiellement au Concile
par le Cardinal Bea qui les reçut directement de l'Ordre B'nai B'rith, maçonnerie
exclusive de juifs, et ceci au mois de juin 1962."

[58] See *AS* III/2, 327-329.

A further addition made reference for the first time to the Muslims, pointing out that they worship the one unique personal God and share common ground with Christians on account of their religious sensitivities and culture.

Cardinal Bea delivered his report on September 25th, an important psychological moment given the fact that the discussion on religious freedom was still in full swing at the time.[59] The report was presented by a German and had the support of the German bishops who made it clear by way of a declaration that the Council represented a sort of examination of conscience for the Catholic Church and that this Church was obliged to make a statement within this context concerning its relationship with the People of God of the Old Testament. The German bishops explicitly grounded their support for the text on the Jews in the injustices committed by the German people against the Jews.[60]

During the debates, which were closely followed by the press, it became clear that a significant majority of the speakers was positively inclined towards the text on the Jews and continued to support its presence on the conciliar agenda.[61] It remains striking, however, that an important group of conciliar fathers called for a return to the text of 1963, which they considered to be more authoritative and more explicit, for example, with respect to the acquittal of the Jews of the accusation of deicide.[62]

Cardinal Ruffini, archbishop of Palermo, caused a degree of consternation when he suggested that while it was correct that one

[59] For the details see Miccoli, "Two Sensitive Issues," 135; 152ff.

[60] As a matter of fact, Bea did not forget to emphasize the fact that a positive attitude towards the Jews was also a component part of the *aggiornamento* intended by John XXIII; cf. *AS* III/2, 564.

[61] For a survey see Miccoli, "Two Sensitive Issues," 159ff.

[62] Bea had already made detailed reference to this matter in his presentation of the text; cf. Miccoli, "Two Sensitive Issues," 153.

should be more friendly towards the Jews — many Jews had been saved from the hands of the Nazis thanks to Catholic initiatives — one also had the right to expect the Jews to be more friendly towards Christians and that they should accordingly remove a number of anti-Christian passages from the Talmud.[63] On behalf of the Eastern patriarchs, Cardinal Tappouni, patriarch of the Syriac Church (Antioch), questioned whether the text was opportune, given that it might occasion political problems for Christians in the Middle East.[64] Other speakers objected that too much attention had been paid to Jews and Muslims to the detriment of other world religions and animism.[65] The latter observations tended to stem from the bishops of sub-Saharan Africa and Asia. Msgr. Heenan, a member of the SCUF, likewise made an important intervention in which he lamented the fact that the text as it now stood lacked the openheartedness of the 1963 text and warned that in the context of ecumenism one should not set out to gain converts but rather to promote mutual understanding.[66] On the suggestion of Cardinal Bea,

[63] Xavier Rynne, *Letters from Vatican City* (London: Faber and Faber, 1965) 3: 42-43.

[64] Cf. *AS* III/2, 582. After the conclusion of discussions in the aula, the bishops from the Middle East continued to evolve a strategy aimed at having the text on the Jews removed from the conciliar agenda; cf. Néophyte Edelby, *Il Vaticano II nel diario di un vescovo arabo*, ed. Riccardo Cannelli (Cinisello Balsamo: San Paolo, 1996) 246-250. Indeed, a text on the Jews not only complicated their position with respect to Islam, it also caused problems for their relations with the Orthodox churches; for further details see Miccoli, "Two Sensitive Issues," 175-176.

[65] See in this regard the intervention of the bishop of Butare (Rwanda), speaking on behalf of roughly 80 colleagues, who insisted that the adherents of animism were sometimes more open to Christianity than Jews and Muslims; see *AS* III/2, 142. For an explanation of this intervention and the list of its signatories see Miccoli, "Two Sensitive Issues," 163-164.

[66] Cf. *AS* III/3, 38. For a discussion of the intervention of Cardinal Lercaro, who emphasized the unique place of the Jews in salvation history, see Miccoli, "Two Sensitive Issues," 161-163.

the chapter on the Jews was included in the schema on Catholic relations with non-Christians. This did not take place without some struggle, however. During a meeting of the presidents of the Coordinating Commission on October 7th 1964, the decision was made after lengthy discussion that the text on the Jews should be included in the schema on the Church (Chapter II, nr. 16).[67] The text to be used for this purpose was to be put together by a mixed commission, consisting of members of the doctrinal commission and the SCUF.[68] Felici informed Bea and Ottaviani of this decision on October 8th.[69] Bea, however, expressed his opposition to the establishment of such a commission.[70]

During a meeting between Cardinals Ottaviani, Bea and Cicognani on November 11th 1964, the decision was made not to include the declaration of the Church's relations with non-Christian religions in the schema on the Church but to publish it later as an appendix thereto.[71] At the end of the third session — on November

[67] Vincenzo Carbone, "Il ruolo di Paolo VI nell'evoluzione e nella redazione della dichiarazione 'Dignitatis Humanae'," in *Paolo VI e il rapporto Chiesa-mondo al Concilio (Colloquio Internazionale di studio, Roma, 22-23-24 settembre 1989)*, Publicazioni dell'Istituto Paolo VI, 11 (Rome: Studium, 1991) 126-176, esp. 135.

[68] See *AS* V/2, 754-757.

[69] See *AS* V/2, 763-765. One may wonder whether it was Felici himself who took the initiative to take away the text *De Judaeis* from the SCUF in order to give it to a mixed commission. Cardinal Alfrink, present at the meeting of the Presidents of the Coordinating Commission on October 7, told Willebrands on October 9 that the meeting of the 7th had not taken clear decisions as suggested by Felici in his letter of October 8. For the details, see now Leo Declerck, *Les Agendas conciliaires de Mgr. J. Willebrands, secrétaire du Secrétariat pour l'Unité des Chrétiens*, Instrumenta Theologica, 31 (Leuven: Peeters, 2009) October 9, 1964.

[70] Cf. *AS* V/2, 779. As will be evident from what follows, Cardinal Bea was to have no difficulties with the submission of the text to the doctrinal commission. Already on October 13, 1964, Bea could inform the SCUF that it remained the only commission competent for both *De libertate religiosa* and *De Judaeis* (Declerck, *Les Agendas conciliaires de Mgr. J. Willebrands*, October 13, 1964).

[71] Cf. *AS* V/3, 62-63; 66-67.

20th 1964 — a vote was finally taken on the attitude of the Church towards non-Christian religions.[72] The new text rejoiced in the title: *Declaratio De Ecclesiae habitudine ad religiones non-christianas*.[73] The section on the Jews was now included within a broader context in which reference was also made (following the foreword) to the other non-Christian religions, including Hinduism and Buddhism (number 2) and a much expanded segment on Islam. Number 4 was devoted to the Jews. From this point onwards, the text on the Jews was to remain in this location. In the first instance, a number of striking emendations of detail should be noted, which can be read as evidence of an increasing degree of benevolence towards the Jewish people and can be understood in part as a return to the 1963 text. Elements of a more positive tone include the explicit reference to Moses, the fact that the rather condescending expression "Paul on the Jews" was replaced by "Paul on his kinsfolk," the inclusion of Rom 9:5 which states that Christ had a bond with the fathers, and the statement insisting that in spite of the recognition of distance between both convictions, Jews remain extremely close to Christians *propter patres*. Furthermore, the emphasis placed on the fact that Jews and Christians share the same spiritual heritage

[72] For a discussion of the plans to give the text on the Jews a place in the schema on the Church see, for example, Congar, *Mon Journal du Concile*, 2: 190; 195; 212-213. Cf. also *AS* V/2, 754-757. (discussion in the Coordinating Commission); see also Miccoli, "Two Sensitive Issues," 166-193, which offers a detailed survey of events surrounding our text and that on religious freedom. The proposal to integrate the text on the Jews into the schema on the Church was ultimately abandoned. On November 12th, 1964, the text as it stood was given the green light by the theological commission: it was thus considered to contain nothing contrary to faith and morals. See in this regard Congar, *Mon Journal du Concile*, 2: 261-262 (with an interesting review of the various antitheses within the theological commission on the said topic).

[73] For the text itself see *AS* III/8, 637-643. The SCUF had already submitted a text on the Jews and the Muslims on October 21st to a small commission consisting of Congar, Stransky (U.S.A.), Neuner (India), Pfister (Japan) and the Belgian Moeller. Congar, *Mon Journal du Concile*, 2: 215-216.

likewise belongs to the same category of positive elements in the text. Moreover, the introduction to number 4 makes explicit reference to the kinship enjoyed by the people of the New Testament with the descendents of Abraham.[74] Where an earlier version of the text had dropped the mention of persecution "then and now," the new text reinstated the reference with full vigor. At the same time, the text explicitly stated anew that the Jewish people as a people should not be condemned or rejected and should not be held responsible as a people for deicide. The text also explicitly stated that the Church adhered to the notion that Christ died *of his own free will* for the sins of all humanity and according to his own inexhaustible love. It is thus a core element of the preaching Church that the cross of Christ be proclaimed as a sign of God's universal love and a source of every grace.

It is interesting to observe that number 33 from the preceding schema had now been significantly abbreviated as the new number 5, that the references to the Jews therein had disappeared and that a short and to the point formulation now made it clear that our love and respect for God was not to be separated from the attitude we take with respect to our fellow human beings. By leaving out the Jewish references, number 5 of the text is given a universalizing conclusion in which the commandment to love God and one's neighbour is extended to include all human beings. Number 34 from the preceding schema, which condemned every form of discrimination, must also be read against this background.

The ballot on numbers 4 and 5 — both were taken together — was a success: 1969 fathers took part, 1770 voted in favor of the text, 185 against and 14 votes were invalid. During the vote on the document as a whole, 1651 votes (out of 1996) were positive,

---

[74] Note that the expression "the people of the New Covenant" had been dropped; cf. *AS* III/8, 640.

242 fathers abstained, and 99 fathers voted against. In other words, the text was broadly approved by the Council participants.

The results of the ballot gave rise to a degree of disapproval, especially from the Arabic nations. For this reason, Bea was to write an article on November 30th in *Osservatore Romano* in which he insisted once again that the text had purely religious motives and that every political interpretation thereof was to be rejected. He considered the fact that the text on the Jews had been integrated in a new text addressed to all the world religions as evidence of its political neutrality. The question of guilt in relation to the ancient accusation of deicide had been treated with the greatest caution: the text had only underlined the fact that the Jews of the Diaspora at the time of Christ as well as the Jews of today bore no guilt whatsoever in this regard. The text was intended in the first instance to contribute to the promotion of peace.[75]

THIRD INTERSESSION

Now that the text had been approved, the Secretariat was expected to evaluate proposed emendations (*modi*). The proposed reintroduction of the word "deicide," called for by an important group of bishops, resulted in renewed protest from the Arabic

[75] See Cottier, "L'historique de la déclaration," 65-67. Cottier also makes reference to the important interventions of Maximos IV Saigh (in an interview) and Heenan (in a sermon in Westminster Cathedral), both of which were inclined in the same direction. He refers, in addition, to the role of Paul VI in helping to restore a sense of calm to the situation. Felici was to react with some bitterness to Bea's article, arguing in a letter to Macchi, private secretary to Paul VI, that no matter how positive the results of the ballot may have been, nothing had in fact been decided; cf. *AS* VI/3, 572. It is evident to the present authors that such a reaction bears witness to an apparent lack of respect for the said results.

world and from more traditional Episcopal circles.[76] The Secretariat of State was far from pleased with the commotion that resulted.[77] It continued to fear that a positive declaration concerning the Jews would necessarily have political implications with respect to the Church's relations with the Arabic nations.[78] Indeed, Bea's article in *Osservatore Romano* referred to above was the result of a request from the Secretary of State Cicognani. In response to the fact that the latter continued to raise problems, Bea sent him a detailed letter on December 23rd 1964, in which he pointed out that the vast majority of the Council fathers had approved the declaration. He likewise noted that protest had already emerged from the Middle East in 1962, long before anyone knew what the text would contain. Bea agreed with Cicognani that it was indeed important to avoid any political interpretation of the declaration, but he insisted at the same time that this had been stated repeatedly during the presentation of the text.[79] Felici was once again of the opinion that additional problems could be avoided if members of the doctrinal commission and the Secretariat for non-Christians would be allowed to participate in the examination of the *modi* and would be given full voting

[76] For what follows see, in particular, Riccardo Burigana and Giovanni Turbanti, "The Intersession: Preparing the Conclusion of the Council," *History of Vatican II*, 4: 546-559.

[77] See in this regard, the letter addressed by Cicognani to Felici, dated December 7th 1964 (*AS* V/3, 96-97). Cf. also *AS* V/3, 104-105.

[78] It remains a fact, moreover, that a number of bishops, especially those from the Middle East, who were against the declaration continued to let their unease in the matter be known in Rome; cf., for example, *AS* VI/3, 628-629; *AS* VI/4, 37; 69; *AS* VI/4, 118. The repudiative attitude of the Orthodox also gave rise to a degree of unrest; cf. *AS* VI/4, 83-85 (letter from Cicognani to Felici, dated February 7th 1965; letter from Felici to Cicognani, dated February 8th 1965).

[79] Letter from Bea to Cicognani, dated December 23rd 1964 (*AS* V/3, 118-120).

rights, just like the members of the SCUF. He asked, in addition, that prior to the completion of the *expensio modorum*, the SCUF's finished work should be submitted as quickly as possible to the pope to allow the latter sufficient time to intervene should he consider it necessary.[80]

In the meantime, sources from the Middle East continued to insinuate that the Catholic Church supported international Zionism and was against the claims of the Palestinians. Protest against the conciliar document even found its way onto the streets. The press campaign conducted by the Arabic papers was likewise considered dangerous for Christians living in this region. The rumor also circulated at the time that the Arabic Catholic communities might join the Orthodox Churches, which were well known in those days for their comparatively anti-Semitic opinions.

It is important to note at this juncture that the Catholic patriarchs of the Middle East expressed their concerns in a constructive manner. This is clearly the case, for example, with respect to the Armenian patriarch, Ignace Pierre XVI Batanian.[81] The Arabic world was in conflict with Israel, a conflict in which no distinction was being made between politics and religion and people were subject to provocation. Public demonstrations were being organized against the Catholic Church and the Council. The positive reactions of the Orthodox with respect to the decree on ecumenism were in danger of being undermined by the proposed declaration on the Jews. Batanian suggested that the schema should be emended in two places. Persecution of whatever people or nation was to be condemned without reservation. Catechesis should avoid every form of

---

[80] Cf. *AS* VI/3, 603-604 (letter from Felici to Cicognani, dated December 16th 1964).

[81] *AS* VI/4, 70-72 (letter to Paul VI, dated January 18th 1965); for additional examples see *AS* VI/4, 73-74.

teaching that might stimulate hatred or contempt towards any nation. The patriarch did not consider special mention of the Jews to be necessary, since other nations, including the Armenians, had also suffered persecution. Christians were to resist every form of discrimination, not only discrimination against the Jews.[82]

In the meantime, the *Coetus Internationalis Patrum*, a group of conservative bishops, kept up the pressure. Cardinal Bea considered himself personally obliged to react to an article published at the beginning of 1965 by Msgr. Carli (bishop of Segni, Italy), one of the driving forces behind the *Coetus Internationalis*. Carli maintained that it was impossible to discuss the Jewish question in a serene manner. In so doing, he transferred the matter to the level of theological reflection. Based on the New Testament, the tradition and the magisterium, he insisted, it was impossible to ignore the guilt of the Jews with respect to the death of Christ, precisely because the Jews had rejected Christ and his message. In other words, the accusation of deicide was theologically correct.[83]

In the meantime, various groups were hard at work on a revision of the schema, first in the sub-commission (from 24th to 28th February 1965) and then in the plenary commission (from 1st to 6th March 1965),[84] endeavouring to account for the 90 proposed emendations submitted by the Council fathers. 32 of the 90 proposals were related to number 4 and 12 of the 32 were upheld. A careful comparison of the text approved in 1964 with the revised text presented in 1965 reveals an agreement of more than 90% with respect to number 4. Recognition of common origin as children of

---

[82] Cf. *AS* VI/4, 71-72.

[83] See Cottier, "L'historique de la déclaration," 71; Burigana and Turbanti, "The Intersession," 548-551.

[84] Cf. *AS* VI/4, 68. On March 3-4, *De Ecclesiae habitudine* was discussed. Cf. Report Willebrands, *Archivio Segreto Vaticano, Fonds Concile Vatican II* (henceforth *ASV Conc. Vat. II*) 1458.

Abraham, respect for the gift of the Old Testament, explicit confirmation of Christ's Jewish roots 'according to the flesh' as son of Mary, as well as those of the apostles and their first followers who proclaimed the gospel to the world remained in the text unabridged. Jews and Christians worshipped one and the same God, and shared a common spiritual heritage that they should cherish and study. The central role of Christ's death in the entirety of the salvation event remained in force. While it was insisted that the gift of the Word did not come from the Jews, the importance of their role as intermediaries therein was beyond dispute. It was to be noted at the same time, however, that the Word revealed itself to all people.[85]

A number of Jews endeavored in the meantime to give the schema a political and Zionist spin. In an Arabic broadcast, for example, Israeli radio made reference to a conciliar acquittal of the Jews on the accusation of deicide. Such reports represented a considerable burden to the activities of the commission[86] and served to explain the impasse that had been reached within the Secretariat at the beginning of March on the question whether the term 'deicide' should be omitted or not omitted.[87] At the same time, Cardinal Bea's efforts to encourage understanding in the Arabic world for the segment on the Jews appeared to have met with little success, given that religion and politics in the said world ultimately went hand in hand.[88] The SCUF pursued many efforts in order to turn the

---

[85] *AS* IV/4, 107.

[86] See in this regard Congar, *Mon Journal du Concile*, 2: 339.

[87] Burigana and Turbanti, "The Intersession," 550. From the perspective of dialogue, the manner with which Paul VI spoke of the Jews during his sermon in the parish church of Nostra Signora di Guadalupe (Rome) on April 4th 1965, occasioned considerable commotion in the Jewish world; cf. Delmaire, "Une ouverture prudente," 822.

[88] Cf. Congar, *Mon Journal du Concile*, 2: 342. Congar also refers to the refusal of the Arabic nations to publicize the Catholic Church's efforts to clarify the precise goal of the declaration via the press or the radio.

tide. Willebrands and Duprey went twice to the Middle East for a visit with Eastern patriarchs. First they visited Lebanon and Syria from March 18 to 23.[89] During a second visit they went to Jordan and Egypt (April 22-30). In a detailed report about this trip,[90] Willebrands describes the tense situation because of the creation of an Israeli state and the loss of property for the Palestinians. For Gori (Latin Patriarch of Jerusalem), this was a sufficient reason to reject any declaration on the Jews. Even proposals to change the text with regard to "deicidium" or the condemnation of anti-Semitism could not change his view. A significant number of Orthodox Christians, among them those of the Coptic Orthodox Church, were opposed to the declaration and supported the Catholics. It was said that Maximos had threatened to leave the council in case the declaration should be approved.[91] Also the Arabic political world was hostile to the declaration: this could lead to a rupture of diplomatic relations and cause much trouble for Arabic Christians.[92] Finally, Willebrands proposed in his report either to change parts of the text or not to promulgate the declaration and consider the text as a guideline for the activities of the SCUF and the Secretariat for the non-Christian religions.[93]

It goes without saying that the meeting of the SCUF of May 9-15 would become a challenging, if not difficult, one.[94] Especially the fact that the pope informed Bea on April 25, 1965 that Maximos was vehemently opposed to the "deicidium" and that in such

[89] With regard to the report of this travel, see *ASV Conc. Vat. II* 1458.

[90] See *AS* V/3, 314-320.

[91] Cf. the report of internuncio Punzolo to Cicognani (March 27, 1965), *ASV Conc. Vat. II* 1458.

[92] See Report Willebrands, 318

[93] Cf. Burigana and Turbanti, "The Intersession," 552. Willebrands already suggested this during his visit to Egypt; Report Willebrands, 317.

[94] Father Long s.j. made a substantial report of the meetings of May 12, 13, and 14. See *ASV Conc. Vat. II* 1458

a context the pope could not promulgate the declaration if that
might result in Maximos leaving the *aula*, complicated things.[95]
In an important intervention of May 12, the bishop of Bruges,
Mgr. De Smedt insisted on the proclamation of the declaration in
the council. He stressed the need to repeat again that the declaration had no political intention – if this might facilitate things, he
suggested to leave out "deicidium" – but asked that the declaration
should clearly state that the whole Jewish people could not be considered responsible for the death of Christ.[96] The meeting was also
very much affected by the intervention of the German bishop
J. Stangl (bishop of Würzburg) who explicitly referred to the geno-
cide.[97]

Finally, the Secretariat decided to omit the term "deicidium."
With regard to the depreciation of anti-Semitism, it was agreed to
replace "damnat" by "deplorat." It was the text with these changes
which would be presented to the council fathers. Indeed, the SCUF
was of the opinion that it was better to have a compromise text
than no text, for, as Congar stated: "Vingt ans après Auschwitz, il
est impossible que le concile ne dise rien."[98] Meanwhile, attempts
should be made to explain more properly the text to the Oriental
bishops and in the Arabic World. This was the immediate cause of
a new visit of Willebrands, De Smedt and Duprey to the Near East
(July 18-24)[99] in order to meet with the patriarchs of the Eastern

---

[95] Cf. *AS* V/3, 211.

[96] Cf. *De Smedt Papers* (Archives of the Centre for the Study of Vatican II,
Maurits Sabbe Library, Faculty of Theology, K.U. Leuven), nr. 1477, inventoried
by Aloïs Greiler and Luc De Saeger, *Emiel-Jozef De Smedt: Papers Vatican II
Inventory*, Instrumenta Theologica, 22 (Leuven: Bibliotheek Godgeleerdheid,
1999) and Report Long, 5-7

[97] Report Long, 9-10; cf. also Burigana and Turbanti, "The Intersession," 566-567.

[98] Cf. Congar, *Mon Journal du Concile*, 2: 366.

[99] For a substantial report of this travel, see *ASV Conc. Vat. II* 1459. Cf. also
Declerck, *Les Agendas conciliaires de Mgr. J. Willebrands*, July 18-24, 1965.

Churches, namely Tappouni (patriarch of the Syriac Church), Meouchi (the Maronite patriarch), Maximos (the Melkite patriarch), Gori (the Latin patriarch), Batanian (the Armenian Patriarch) and Sidarouss (patriarch of the Copts). The primary purpose of the visit was to discuss whether such a text on the Jews was opportune or necessary. The visit appears to have been a success.[100] With the exception of the Latin patriarch, Gori,[101] who continued to raise ecumenical and political objections, all of the others finally approved the text[102] and were prepared to defend it in the event of difficulties.[103] On September 27-28, the embassies of the Arabic nations were informed of the discussion. Surprisingly enough,[104] however, the same cannot be said for the commission members of the SCUF.[105] Moreover, during his meeting with the three Roman

---

[100] Congar, *Mon Journal du Concile*, 2: 392.

[101] See his letter to Cicognani, dated August 10th 1965 (*AS* VI/4, 405-407). Gori appears to have been someone who stubbornly held on to his own convictions. This is apparent, among other things, from the fact that he continued to raise problems after the declaration had been approved in October, 1965, with respect to the use of Rom 11:28 in the text, for example. When it appeared that Bea was refusing to make any changes to the text on account of the ballot results, Gori had the audacity to say: "Je ne puis vraiment m'empêcher de penser qu'un tel procédé est peu digne d'un texte conciliaire et je m'en étonne d'un exégète de la classe de Votre Éminence." (*AS* V/3, 513).

[102] Cf. Leo Declerck and André Haquin (eds.), *Mgr. Albert Prignon, Recteur du Pontificio Collegio Belga: Journal conciliaire de la 4e Session.* Préface de Mgr. Aloys Jousten. Introduction par Claude Troisfontaines, Cahiers de la Revue théologique de Louvain, 35 (Louvain-la-Neuve: Faculté de théologie, 2003) 269.

[103] Congar, *Mon Journal du Concile*, 2: 393-394.

[104] Evidence that periti such as Charles Moeller tended to be lacking in optimism at the beginning of the fourth session has to do in part with the fact that these emendations had only been presented on September 15th and that they had to be accepted without much discussion. Cf. Declerck and Haquin (eds.), *Journal Prignon*, 33-34.

[105] For further details on the said visit see, for example, De Smedt Papers, Greiler and De Saeger, *Emiel-Jozef De Smedt*, nos. 1473-1474.

emissaries, Maximos IV proposed four minor[106] emendations that should be included in the text without discussion in the SCUF. While this is easy to comprehend in light of the threats made during the first visit and the respect enjoyed by Maximos at the Council and in the press, it nevertheless ran counter to the customary procedures of a commission. The first emendation was a question of nuance: it would be wrong to hold all the Jews of Jesus' time responsible without distinction (*indistinctim*) for the death of Christ. The second emendation — in the same section — *Licet autem Ecclesia sit novus populus Dei* represented an accentuation of the idea that the Church was the new people of God. The text was made more restrictive at this juncture than had been the case in the previous version. A third addition was intended to make clear that the Church condemned every form of persecution, including that of the Jews. The patriarch concluded with a request that the Scriptural reference that spoke of "*carissimi manent* (the Jews) *propter patres*" (Rom 11:28) ought to be dropped because the first half of the same verse speaks of the Jews as "*inimici secundum evangelium.*" The patriarch was correct in pointing out in this regard that reference to the second part of the verse while omitting the first part was ultimately an abuse of Paul's text.[107] At the same time, however, a change of attitude could be observed with respect to Maximos IV. Indeed, he was to completely support the

---

[106] This, at any rate, was the opinion of Msgr. De Smedt on the matter; cf. Declerck and Haquin (eds.), *Journal Prignon*, 269.

[107] For the text of Maximos IV, see Greiler and De Saeger, *Emiel-Jozef De Smedt*, no. 1475. For the letter of Maximos to Bea (July 26, 1965), see *ASV Conc. Vat. II* 1459. For the revised text, which took account of Maximos' critique — the first clause has been reformulated — while simultaneously preserving the "carissimi" idea see *AS* IV/4, 707-708; the fourth amendment was rejected; inaccurately, Congar, *Mon Journal du Concile*, 2: 92 makes reference to three *modi*.

declaration during the fourth session, a far from insignificant fact given his authority within the Council as a whole.

It has to be recognized, nevertheless, that from a progressive standpoint some of the emendations in question appeared to undermine the strength of the *Textus approbatus*. Where the *Textus approbatus* stated that the Church was mindful of the ties that bound it to the people of Abraham, the definitive text spoke of the ties whereby the Church "was spiritually bound to the people of Abraham."[108] The passage in which the Jewish people were acquitted of deicide is reduced to the statement that the death of Christ ought not to be ascribed *en masse* to the Jews of Jesus' day and certainly not to the Jews of today. Any explicit reference to the acquittal of the Jews on the charge of deicide has disappeared from the definitive text.[109] Lacking in the preceding text, the addition "Although the Church is the new people of God" serves to undermine the statement that the Jews should no longer be considered rejected by God. The word 'although' bears considerable weight in this statement.

While the *Textus approbatus* continued to forcefully condemn every form of injustice against humanity, the new text offered a much weakened statement by omitting the verb *damnat*: "Moreover, the Church, which condemns all persecutions against any people, mindful of its common inheritance with the Jews and motivated not by political considerations but by the religious charity of the gospel, deplores — and here lies the point of contention, since the verb 'condemns' is omitted —, feelings of hatred, persecutions and demonstrations of anti-Semitism directed against the Jews at whatever time and by whomsoever."[110]

[108] *AS* IV/4, 693.

[109] *Ibid.*

[110] Burigana and Turbanti, "The Intersession," 552ff. suggest that Paul VI himself was significantly involved in this decision. The pope did not want the term *damnat* to be employed in a conciliar text. In spite of considerable pressure

On the other hand, it ought to be noted that certain emendations clearly reinforce the declaration. The text "As Holy Scripture testifies, Jerusalem did not know the time of its visitation, and for the most part the Jews did not accept the gospel, indeed many of them opposed its dissemination," for example, sounds considerably less blunt than the original "a large number of the Jews did not accept the gospel."[111]

The historian is left with the impression that the Secretariat ultimately opted for what was possible. At the same time, he or she is fully aware that in light of the circumstances in the Middle East at the time, there was little if any alternative.

FOURTH SESSION

On September 15th 1965, the SCUF rounded off its activities in a plenary meeting. By the end of the same month, the definitive text and the *Expensio modorum* had been distributed in the aula with a view to obtaining final approval of the material as a whole.[112] The *Expensio* had been implemented with the greatest of care. It also has to be stated that the majority of the *modi* exhibited a sympathetic undertone and were happily included in the reopening of discussions. *Modi* that were critical towards the text — a not insignificant number continued to call for a greater emphasis on the difference between Christians and Jews — were carefully studied,

---

from the *Coetus Internationalis Patrum*, a *damnatio* was likewise avoided with respect to communism.

[111] *AS* IV/4, 694.

[112] Cf. *AS* IV/4, 690-725; for the *Expensio modorum*, cf. 705ff. The *Expensio* clearly reveals that the SCUF did not intend to offer a complete treatment of the other world religions with the text it presented, its goal being rather to propose only practical and pastoral norms that, based on revelation, might be necessary for engaging in dialogue and cooperating with other religions; cf. *AS* IV/4, 706.

provided with detailed commentary and on occasion integrated into the text. The majority thereof, however, were rejected.[113]

Those who opposed the said declaration and the arguments they employed had remained more or less the same since the period of the first text. The more conservative bishops continued to be against any openness towards non-Christian religions. On the other hand, a smaller group of bishops continued to have problems with the omission of words such as 'deicide' and 'condemnation' because they considered their absence to weaken the text. The Arabic world also continued to let its voice be heard, offering mainly political critique with regard to the segment on the Jews, which it considered to be pro-Israel in political terms.

On October 11th, a few days before the ballot on the emendation of the text, the *Coetus Internationalis Patrum* distributed a document in which it called for the rejection of the schema with a *non placet* vote.[114] The document could be described as polemical towards the SCUF. The results of the ballot during the third session were called into question because the signatories were of the opinion that the text had been presented too late, namely with only two days for discussion *in aula*. It was suggested, moreover, that the SCUF had not been objective enough in its examination of proposed corrections. The *Coetus* was also unable to accept that the Jewish people had been acquitted *in globo* on the charge of deicide.

---

[113] *AS* IV/4, 707-708.

[114] A letter from Msgr. Lefebvre (General of the Spiritans), Msgr. Sigaud (Diamantina, Brazil) and Msgr. Carli, leading members of the *Coetus*, dated July 25th 1965 (*AS* VI/4, 373-374), makes it clear that the group was not particularly in tune with conciliar regulations. In light of the results of the vote (more than 80% of the fathers had given their approval to the text, in spite of its delicate nature, so that only the *modi* were still open for discussion), their request to work further with majority and minority *relatores* is strange to say the least, especially with respect to the segment on non-Christian religions.

As we know, the segment of the text concerning the Jews (number 4) had been further subdivided into four parts with a view to the forthcoming vote. While the three remaining points were acceptable, the point referring to the acquittal of the Jews was still considered objectionable. The *Coetus'* most significant difficulties were to be located within numbers 1-3, which fall outside the theme of the present contribution.[115] The core of their objection was that appreciation for other world religions could lead to the equalization of all religions. Furthermore, it had the potential to call into question every form of missionary activity.[116]

It also continues to be remarkable that, in the days prior to the vote in Rome, the fathers were regularly bombarded with anti-Semitic pamphlets, one of which was signed by no less than 21 traditionalist organizations. The fact that both John XXIII and Paul VI had appealed for dialogue and study in the matter makes such activities all the more surprising.[117] Objections can also be raised with respect to the tone of the pamphlets in question: bishops who voted yes were to be branded as heretics; the Council lacked the authority to change the anti-Semitic stance of the Church's magisterium.[118] Certain parties even went so far as to threaten in a letter to Cardinal Marella to blow up Saint Peter's if the segment on the Jews was approved!

The text was subjected to the vote of the Council on October 14th and 15th 1965. Four questions were posed with respected to number 4 in line with the four most important principles in the document: common heritage, rejection of collective responsibility on

---

[115] Mauro Velati, "Completing the Conciliar Agenda," *History of Vatican II*, 5: 211-221.

[116] See in this regard Rynne, *Letters from Vatican City*, 5: 170-171.

[117] One is left with the impression that a number of journals that found their way onto this list did so without their own knowledge or indeed approval; cf. the letter from De Castro Mayer to Felici, dated October 16th 1965 (*AS* VI/4, 562).

[118] Velati, "Completing the Conciliar Agenda," 214-215.

the question of deicide; attitude to the Jewish people in the context of catechesis; rejection of anti-Semitism with an appeal to the universal love of Christ.

It deserves to be stated that the SCUF not only studied every remark introduced concerning the declaration with great care, it also made every effort to reduce the tensions that had arisen as a result of the text via its various contacts abroad and the visits outlined above.[119] In the month of September 1965, for example, a press office was established for the Arabic world that had provided a translation and explanation of the document in Arabic. The latter was distributed on October 6th and accompanied by a lengthy presentation.[120] With the exception of the Iraqi embassy, reactions were positive.[121] Willebrands received a Palestinian delegation who made it clear that they did not wish to engage in a war with the Holy See, a sentiment that was confirmed by the Arabic bishops. Patriarch Maximos published a text in which the Melkite synod expressed its appreciation for the text. The latter also ensured that everything was made ready in the Middle East to present the document in a positive manner to the Arabic world immediately after the vote. The pope's visit to the UNO had likewise elicited a considerable degree of good will among the Arabic nations.[122]

As was often the case, however, protest was also to be registered from within certain Jewish circles who opposed the changes that had been introduced.[123]

[119] For a thorough and detailed survey of both the initiatives stemming from the SCUF and the evolution among the Arabs in the Middle East see AS V/3, 440-442.

[120] Cf. Edelby, Il Vaticano II nel diario, 309.

[121] See AS V/3, 440.

[122] AS V/3, 441-442.

[123] For this and other protests, including those from the United States, see Velati, "Completing the Conciliar Agenda," 216ff.

Given the fact that the text had in fact been approved as such in 1964, there was nothing further to be done than to follow the procedure and move on to the voting stage. This took place on October 14th, after Bea had delivered his report of the activities of the SCUF in the matter. He pointed out that the SCUF had taken its responsibilities seriously and that it had maintained the criteria of clarity and intelligibility throughout its deliberations.[124] Bea repeated with respect to number 4 that every endeavor had been made to explain the theological scope of the document and insisted once again that the schema enjoyed an exclusively religious character. In other words, any political interpretation of the document was to be rejected.[125] With respect to this latter point, the SCUF had explicitly stated in its text that the "church (...), mindful of its common inheritance with the Jews and motivated not by political considerations but by the religious charity of the gospel, deplores feelings of hatred, persecutions and demonstrations of anti-Semitism directed against the Jews at whatever time and by whomsoever." The SCUF hoped that this statement would undermine any effort to give the text a political spin. On the question of Jewish responsibility for deicide, the new text — "the Jewish authorities with their followers pressed for the death of Christ" — was intended to make it clear that an effort had been made to remain faithful to the truth of the gospel while excluding the unjust condemnation of all Jews. All those charged with catechesis and preaching were to respect this evangelical truth and the Spirit of Christ in their activities. The omission of the word "deicide" from the text was justified on the basis of the fact that the word as such already ran counter to the gospel. Moreover, the new formulation

---

[124] For the *relatio* in question see *AS* IV/4, 722-724.

[125] Cf. *AS* IV/4, 723: "Ut natura exclusive *religiosa* schematis clare exprimeretur, ita ut omni ope via ad quamcumqe interpretationem politicam praecluderetur."

already stated explicitly that the Jews were not all responsible for the death of Christ. As John XXIII had insisted, pastoral care and Christian charity were to be given priority in the matter. Bea concluded by expressing his hope that the fathers would share these concerns.[126]

Given the circumstances, the vote with respect to number 4 was to be described as a success. A comfortable majority was achieved for all four elements of the text, although it cannot be ignored that 245 fathers still voted against the text presented to them on the question of the condemnation of the Jews. While this number was significant, it remains relative if one considers that 1,821 fathers approved of the formulation as tabled.[127] The result of the vote elicited positive reactions from the World Council of Churches, for example, and the president of the American Jewish Committee.[128] On the other hand, the Greek Orthodox patriarch Theodosius condemned the approval for his part as an attack on the foundations of Christianity.[129]

It seems far from redundant to underline the fact once again at this juncture that the document on the Jews was ultimately addressed to Christians and not Jews. The goal of the document was to put an end to every form of anti-Semitism within Christianity.

---

[126] *AS* IV/4, 724.

[127] It is evident from the letters written by Cardinals Shehan (Baltimore) and Journet to the pope (referring to the disappointment of Jacques Maritain on the matter), dated October 14th (*AS* V/3, 425-427) that some of those who had voted yes also lamented the omission of the word "damnat" from number 4. Shehan's letter in particular provides detailed motivation. Given the fact that the text had been approved, the SCUF was no longer at liberty to introduce the proposed changes; cf. the letter of Bea to Cicognani, dated October 22nd (*AS* V/3, 470).

[128] As a matter of fact, Cardinal Bea did not hesitate to pass on both their letters of congratulation to the pope within days of the vote (October 16th; cf. *AS* V/3, 438-440).

[129] Velati, "Completing the Conciliar Agenda," 222, n. 98.

It also desired to give expression to the fact that Christians consider themselves indebted to the Jews to a considerable degree. It can be lamented, together with several of the bishops, that the text in its final version represented a cautious, perhaps over-cautious statement. At the same time, however, it would be exaggerated to suggest that the text on the Jews was dramatically enfeebled. Indeed, one should not forget that the Council endeavored to achieve the highest possible unanimity and in doing so it was constantly obliged to steer a middle path. It is a well known fact that the majority, on occasion, was likewise obliged to acquiesce to the opinions of the minority. In spite of this, it cannot be denied that the Church of Vatican II ultimately opened a new chapter in its attitude towards the Jews with the presentation and approval of the text under discussion.

In order to be sure that the text would be promulgated, Msgr. De Smedt and other members of the SCUF explicitly asked Cardinal Suenens and the other moderators to request that the pope promulgate the text prior to October 28th or at least make an announcement that the text's promulgation was to be expected. It was evident that the fear of renewed difficulties from both Jewish and Arabic quarters continued to be a cause for concern.[130] As a matter of fact, a similar initiative was undertaken by Cardinal Bea.[131] The declaration was definitively approved on October 28th. 2312 fathers took part in the vote. 2221 voted *placet*, 88 *non placet*, 2 *placet juxta modum* and 1 vote was invalid.

Nostra Aetate was a fact. Although some engaged in a number of rearguard actions after October 28th, no further changes were possible. The time had come to move on to the period of implementation.

---

[130] Declerck and Haquin (eds.), *Journal Prignon*, 171-172.
[131] Letter from Bea dated October 16th (*AS* V/3, 439).

CONCLUSION

The purpose of the schema was clear from the outset: the establishment of a position on anti-Semitism and a reflection on the part of the Church on its own Jewish roots. As the text evolved through its various versions, both concerns continued to be preserved.

It remains a pity, of course, that a definitive statement on the question of deicide was omitted from the definitive text. One can also lament the fact that pastoral concern, much more evident in the first draft, had lost much of its vigor by the time of the definitive text.[132] At the same time, however, it is important to point out that the inclusion of the text on the Jews within a broader declaration on non-Christian religions ultimately ensured, at least in part, that the Council was able to make a statement on the Jews. Indeed, the broader context served to facilitate the matter to a significant degree. The final declaration created a space both in breadth and in depth within the Roman Catholic Church for genuine inter-religious dialogue. As a matter of fact, it continues to be one of the SCUF's greatest achievements that this document and the document on religious freedom were able to initiate a genuine *aggiornamento* within the Roman Catholic Church on such important and delicate matters.[133]

The history of *Nostra Aetate* teaches us that the matter was evidently a sensitive one in the Middle East. At the same time, it reveals that those who opposed the declaration did so because their theological formation had clearly presented them with different, anti-Semitic convictions. Their appeal to the tradition may have

---

[132] See in this regard Mauro Velati, "La proposta ecumenica del segretariato per l'unità dei cristiani," *Verso il Concilio Vaticano II (1960-1962): Passagi e problemi della preparazione conciliare*, ed. Guiseppe Alberigo and Alberto Melloni, Istituto per le scienze religiose di Bologna. Testi e ricerche di scienze religiose, 11 (Genova: Marietti,1993) 331-337.

[133] Cf. Delmaire, "Une ouverture prudente," 825ff.

been justified, but it simultaneously exposed the fact that they had been blind to new developments. Perhaps of greater importance to such an observation, however, is the fact that the declaration on the Jews — together with the declaration on religious freedom — made it clear that the Roman Catholic Church was ultimately capable of setting aside ancient traditions where sound biblical, historical and cultural arguments insisted upon it.

REFLECTIONS ON COVENANT AND MISSION FORTY YEARS AFTER *NOSTRA AETATE*

John T. PAWLIKOWSKI

The release of the study document *Reflections on Covenant and Mission* from an ongoing consultation between the National Council of Synagogues in the USA and the U.S. Catholic Bishops' Committee on Ecumenical and Interreligious Affairs on 12 August 2002,[1] caused a firestorm in sectors of the Catholic Church with Cardinal Avery Dulles taking a lead in attacking the document.[2] While no single document within mainline Protestantism has elicited quite the same vigorous response, a number of European statements such as the declaration from the Rhineland Synod[3] in Germany have elicited strong reactions. And some evangelical Protestant groups in the United States have severely critiqued

---

[1] Cf. Bishops' Committee on Ecumenical and Interreligious Affairs and the National Council of Synagogues, "Reflections on Covenant and Mission," *Origins* 32 (2002) 218-224. In a recent volume Cardinal Edward Idris Cassidy describes this document as an important challenge for the church. Cf. Edward Idris Cassidy, *Recovering Vatican II: Ecumenism and Interreligious Dialogue* (Mahwah, NJ: Paulist Press, 2005) 252-256.

[2] Cf. Avery Dulles, "Evangelization and the Jews," with a Response by Mary Boys. In Philip Cunningham and John Pawlikowski, *America* 187 (2002) 8-16.

[3] Cf. "Towards Renovation of the Relationship of Christians and Jews: A Statement of the Evangelical Church of the Rhineland," *The Theology of the Churches and the Jewish People: Statements by the World Council of Churches and its Member Churches*, ed. Allen Brockway, Paul van Buren, Rolf Rendtorff and Simon Schoon (Geneva: WCC Publications, 1988) 92-94. Also cf. Hannah Holdtschneider, *The 1980 Statement of the Rhineland Synod: A Landmark in Christian-Jewish Relations in Germany* (Cambridge, UK: OJCR Press, 2002).

several statements, including the recent Pontifical Biblical Commission document dealing with the Jews and their Scriptures in the New Testament and the statement *A Sacred Obligation* released in September 2002 by the ecumenical Christian Scholars Group on Christian-Jewish Relations. Clearly the discussion of the theology of the Jewish-Christian relationship and its implication for the churches' understanding of mission relative to the Jews has moved center stage in recent years. We shall return to the contemporary discussion later in this essay. But first a bit of recent history on the question is in order.

In an address to the Catholic Theological Society of America annual meeting in 1986, the Canadian theologian Gregory Baum, who served as an expert at the Second Vatican Council and worked on *Nostra Aetate*, argued that "the Church's recognition of the spiritual status of the Jewish religion is the most dramatic example of doctrinal turn-about in the age-old magisterium ordinarium" to occur at the Council.[4] For centuries Christian theology, beginning with most of the major Church Fathers in the second century and thereafter, was infected with a viewpoint which saw the Church as replacing 'old' Israel in the covenantal relationship with God. This replacement theology relegated Jews to a miserable and marginal status which could only be overcome through conversion.[5]

Vatican II's *Nostra Aetate*, together with many parallel Protestant documents, fundamentally changed Christianity's theological posture relative to Jews and Judaism that had permeated its

[4] Gregory Baum, "The Social Context of American Catholic Theology," *Proceedings of the Catholic Theological Society of America* 41 (1986) 87.

[5] Cf. Eamon Flannery, *The Anguish of the Jews* (New York: Macmillan, 1965). Cf. also Marvin Perry and Frederick Schweitzer (eds.), *Antisemitism: Myth and Hate — From Antiquity to the Present* (New York: Palgrave/Macmillan, 2002). Cf. also John Pawlikowski, *Sinai and Calvary: A Meeting of Two Peoples* (Beverly Hills, CA: Benzinger, 1976) 129-161.

theology, art, and practice for nearly eighteen hundred years. Jews were now to be seen as integral to the ongoing divine covenant. Jesus and early Christianity were portrayed as deeply rooted in a constructive sense in the religiosity of Second Temple Judaism (particularly its Pharisaic branch). Jews were not to be held collectively accountable for the death of Jesus. Vatican II did not 'forgive' Jews of the so-called crime of deicide as some newspaper headlines proclaimed. Rather it argued that there existed no basis for such a charge in the first place.

One indication of how thorough the change was on the Catholic side can be seen in the references the bishops at Vatican II used to support their argument for a basic turn in the Church's understanding of its relationship with the Jewish people. Eugene Fisher, who oversees Catholic-Jewish relations for the United States Conference of Catholic Bishops, wrote some years ago that "*Nostra Aetate*, for all practical purposes, begins the Church's teaching (...) concerning a theological or, more precisely, a doctrinal understanding of the relationship between the Church as 'People of God' and 'God's People' Israel."[6] Examining paragraph four of *Nostra Aetate* we find scarcely any reference to the usual sources cited in conciliar documents: the Church Fathers, papal statements and previous conciliar documents. Rather, the Declaration returns to Romans 9–11, as if to say that the Church is now taking up where Paul left off in his insistence that Jews remain part of the covenant after the Resurrection despite the theological ambiguity involved in such a statement. Without saying it so explicitly, the 2221 Council members who voted for *Nostra Aetate* were in fact stating that

---

[6] Eugene Fisher, "The Evolution of a Tradition: From *Nostra Aetate* to the *Notes*. International Catholic-Jewish Liaison Committee," *Fifteen Years of Catholic-Jewish Dialogue: 1970-1985* (Rome: Libreria Editrice Vaticana/Libreria Editrice Lateranense, 1988) 239.

everything that had been said about the Christian-Jewish relationship since Paul moved in a direction they could no longer support.
It is interesting to note that *Nostra Aetate* never makes reference
to the several passages in the Letter to the Hebrews where the original covenant appears to be abrogated after Christ and the Jewish
law overturned (Heb 7:12; 8:13 and 10:9). Given the interpretive
role of a Church Council in the Catholic tradition this omission is
theologically significant. It indicates that the Council Fathers
judged these texts from Hebrews as a theologically inappropriate
resource for thinking about the relationship between Christianity
and Judaism today. I will return to this point subsequently in discussing Cardinal Avery Dulles' reaction to the study document
Reflections on Covenant and Mission.

In reality the theological about-face on the Jews at Vatican II
represents, along with such closely related statements as the affirmation of the democratic constitutional state in the *Declaration on
Religious Liberty* and the depiction of the Catholic Church as 'sub-
sisting' in the one true Church in which the other Christian
churches are to be regarded as integral members in the document
on ecumenism, one of the central theological developments at the
Council. Unfortunately its full significance for all of Christianity
has been insufficiently recognized up till now within Catholicism.
This is also largely true within Protestantism where the several
ground-breaking statements on continued Jewish covenantal inclusion have not significantly impacted the course of Christian theological reflection in the last forty years.

The German theologian Johann Baptist Metz is one Christian
scholar who acknowledged the overall theological implications of
the recent documents from the Christian churches on the understanding of the Christian-Jewish relationship. Metz has insisted that
these implications go far beyond the parameters of the Christian-
Jewish dialogue. Especially after the Holocaust, Metz insists, they

involve a "revision of Christian theology itself."[7] Yet we have seen little impact from these documents thus far on theology as such. One looks in vain for citations to *Nostra Aetate* and subsequent papal/Vatican documents on Christian-Jewish relations or to the major parallel Protestant statements in books or documents reflecting on Christian theological identity outside the context of the dialogue with Jews. Yet, historically, Christian identity, including in particular Christological affirmation, has been rooted in the notion of the Church as the replacement for the Jewish people in the covenantal relationship with God.

Jewish participants in the dialogue with Christians have sometimes noted the above reality with dismay. They are right in expressing their concern. Do these declarations on the Church's relationship with the Jewish people have relevance only when Christians are actually speaking with Jews? Or are they brought into the picture when Christians are conversing among themselves in terms of theological identity. Only if we begin to see a development of the latter can we say that there has been genuine reception of *Nostra Aetate* and the Protestant declarations within the Christian community.

Let me cite two examples where I have seen a failure to understand the profound implications of *Nostra Aetate* and similar Protestant statements. The first was in the process leading up to the international ecumenical gathering held at Santiago de Compostela, Spain, several years ago. In the preparatory drafts of the major statement to be issued from that gathering the vision of Christian self-identity was dangerously close to displacement theology. Yet little objection was initially raised to this perspective

---

[7] Johann Baptist Metz, "Facing the Jews: Christian Theology after Auschwitz," *The Holocaust as Interruption*, ed. Elisabeth Schüssler-Fiorenza and David Tracy; Concilium, 175 (Edinburgh: T & T Clark, 1984) 27.

either by Protestant or Catholic church leaders involved with the process until some of us connected with Christian-Jewish dialogue raised a fuss. Eventually the final document was altered to back away from the displacement theme. But I cannot say the final document fully embodied the full implications of the recent Christian statements on the Church's relationship to the Jewish people. For me this experience continued to illustrate how far we still are from integrating the recent documents on Christian-Jewish relations into mainstream Christian theological thinking.

A second example occurred during the October 1997 meeting at the Vatican on the Church and anti-Judaism. I was one of three American scholars participating in this meeting, part of the Vatican's preparation for the new millennium and specifically for the anticipated papal apology for anti-Semitism which took place on the first Sunday of Lent, 2000, and shortly thereafter during the papal visit to Jerusalem. Throughout the meeting I was often dismayed at the lack of acquaintance with the theological vision of *Nostra Aetate* displayed by some of the participants, including high curial officials. One bishop argued that the primary purpose of the Jewish people from a religious perspective was to teach Christians how to suffer. This gathering further convinced me that much work remains if the profound implications of chapter four of *Nostra Aetate* are to be realized within Catholicism and lead to the about-face in Christian theology that Gregory Baum saw them as inaugurating.

Nostra Aetate and the concomitant Protestant documents have given rise to several attempts by theologians to restate the basic understanding of Christianity's relationship to Judaism. I have summarized these theological developments in a number of my own writings.[8] They include: (1) an appreciation that the Jewish

---

[8] Cf. John Pawlikowski, *Christ in the Light of Christian-Jewish Dialogue* (Eugene, OR: Wipf and Stock, 2001); *Jesus and the Theology of Israel*

covenant remains valid after the coming of Christ; (2) Christianity is not automatically superior to Judaism, nor is it the simple fulfillment of Judaism as traditionally claimed; (3) the Sinai covenant is, in principle, as crucial to Christian faith expression as is the covenant in Christ. There was no 'old' Testament for Jesus and there should not be for us; and (4) Christianity needs to reincorporate dimensions from its original Jewish matrix in a central way in its contemporary faith expression.

I realize that most, if not all of these assertions, may appear controversial to many. But I believe they are demanded by the revolution in theological thinking about the Christian-Jewish relationship represented by chapter four of *Nostra Aetate* and its companion documents from the Protestant churches. To repeat the point made by Metz, the new theological understanding of the Jewish-Christian relations affects the basic face of Christian theology. That it may also do so with respect to Jewish theological self-understanding is something upon which Jewish scholars need to reflect. Some have begun that process as the recent Jewish statement on Christianity *Dabru Emet* and its accompanying theological volume have shown.[9]

As some Christian theologians moved to reexamine Christianity's theological understanding of Judaism just prior to and following Vatican II they tended to focus on Paul's reflections on the post-Easter Jewish-Christian relationship which he articulated in

(Wilmington, DE: Michael Glazier, 1989); "Christology, Anti-Semitism, and Christian-Jewish Bonding," *Reconstructing Christian Theology*, ed. Rebecca Chopp and Mark Lewis Taylor (Minneapolis, MN: Fortress Press, 1994); and "The Christ Event and the Jewish people," *Thinking of Christ: Proclamation, Explanation, Meaning*, ed. Tatha Wiley (New York/London: Continuum, 2003) 103-121.

[9] *Dabru Emet* can be found (with commentaries by Jewish and Christians scholars) in Tikva Frymer-Kensky, David Novak, Peter Ochs, David Fox Sandmel, and Michael Signer (eds.), *Christianity in Jewish Terms* (Boulder, CO: Westview Press, 2000).

Romans 9–11. These chapters, as was already indicated, served as the basis for Vatican II's approach to the Jewish-Christian issue. And they have been central to Protestant re-evaluations as well, including the recent statement from the Leuenberg Fellowship of Reformation Churches in Europe.

The first generation of Christian scholars dealing with this issue saw a basis in these Pauline chapters' assertion that God remains faithful to the original people of the covenant for their pioneering efforts to rethink the meaning of Christology, at least in terms of the insistence that 'newness' in Christ cannot be stated in a manner that relegates Jews to covenantal removal. Some of these pioneering scholars, after considerable reflection, were forced to conclude that it is not possible for the Church to go beyond saying what Paul himself said, *i.e.*, that reconciliation between an assertion of redemptive 'newness' in Christ and the concomitant affirmation of the continued participation of the Jewish people in the ongoing covenant remains a 'mystery' presently understandable to God. Only at the end time might we come to see the lack of contradiction in these twin theological statements. Associated with this line of thought were scholars such as Kurt Hruby, Jacques Maritain and Jean Daniélou. This was also the perspective of Cardinal Augustine Bea who initially was suspicious of such new theological thinking about the Christian-Jewish relationship,[10] but eventually came to play a central role in Vatican II's approval of *Nostra Aetate* and organized the initial implementation of the statement immediately following the close of the Council.

These early attempts to eradicate a Christology rooted in Jewish covenantal displacement continued to insist on a central role for

[10] Michael Phayer, *The Catholic Church and the Holocaust, 1930-1965* (Bloomington, IN/Indianapolis, IN: Indiana University Press, 2000) 206-215.

Christ in all human salvation as well as on a fulfillment dimension in Jesus' incarnation and resurrection. No effort was made to erase the apparent contradiction between the affirmation of Jewish covenantal continuity and fulfillment in Christ. Rather these scholars argued for a dual proclamation of Jewish covenantal inclusion and salvific fulfillment in Christ as integral to Christian faith expression.

In these scholars' perspective God remains sovereign both of Jews and Christians. Therein is to be found the basis for the reconciliation of these two seemingly contradictory assertions. As we shall see subsequently, this tension is far from overcome even in more recent theological attempts at stating the theology of the Christian-Jewish relationship from the side of the Church.

Scripture scholars in particular have played a major role in the process of revising Christianity's theological approach to Judaism. We are in the midst of a genuine revolution in New Testament and early Christian scholarship, as well as parallel scholarship on the Judaism, or as some scholars such as Jacob Neusner would prefer it, the 'Judaisms' of the time. Within Christian biblical scholarship the dominance of the 'Religionsgeschichte' approach, found in Rudolf Bultmann especially but also some of his disciples such as Ernst Käsemann and Helmut Koester, has significantly receded. This exegetical framework seriously undercut any notion of Jesus' concrete ties to, and dependence upon, biblical and Second Temple Judaism. This in turn tended to produce an excessively universalistic interpretation of Jesus' message which harbored the seeds of theological anti-Judaism and reinforced the traditional supersessionist interpretation of the Christian-Jewish relationship.

There have been a number of leading biblical scholars, some with a continuing transcontinental influence, who have contributed to the removal of Judaism from the heart of the Christian faith, an

66 JOHN T. PAWLIKOWSKI

image that has been central to Pope John Paul II's numerous writings on Christianity and Judaism.[11] One of the most prominent has been Gerhard Kittel, the original editor of the widely used *Theological Dictionary of the New Testament*.[12] Kittel viewed postbiblical Jews as forming a community in dispersion. "Authentic Judaism," he wrote, "abides by the symbol of the stranger wandering restless and homeless on the face of the earth."[13] And the prominent exegete Martin Noth, whose *History of Israel* became a standard reference for students and professors alike, spoke of Israel as a strictly "religious community" which experienced a slow, agonizing death in the first century C. E. Noth argues that Jewish history reached its culmination in the arrival of Jesus: "Jesus himself no longer formed part of the history of Israel. In him the history of Israel had come, rather, to its real end. What did belong to the history of Israel was the process of his rejection and condemnation by the Jerusalem religious community."[14] After this condemnation the history of Israel moved quickly to its end.

The implication of Noth's perspective is that the Jewish people and its tradition no longer have a role to play in the Church's theological understanding of Jesus' ministry. Such a view has not altogether disappeared in Christianity, even if redefined within a wider global context. Prominent Asian Christian theologian Wesley

[11] Cf. Eugene Fisher and Leon Klenicki (eds.), *Pope John Paul II on Jews and Judaism* (Washington, DC: United States Catholic Conference, 1987) and Eugene Fisher and Leon Klenicki (eds.), *Spiritual Pilgrimage: Texts on Jews and Judaism 1979-1995-Pope John Paul II* (New York: Crossroad, 1995). Also cf. Byron Sherwin and Harold Kasimow (eds.), *John Paul II and Interreligious Dialogue* (Maryknoll, NY: Orbis, 1999).

[12] Gerhard Kittel, *Die Judenfrage* (Stuttgart: Kohlhammer, 1933) 73.

[13] Martin Noth, *The Law in the Pentateuch and Other Stories* (Edinburgh: Oliver and Boyd, 1966).

[14] Rudolf Bultmann, *Theology of the New Testament* (New York: Scribner's, 1951).

Ariarajah who worked for many years in the interreligious office of the World Council of Churches recently termed the effort to return Jesus to his Jewish context in such documents as *A Sacred Obligation* a "futile attempt" in terms of creating Christian faith expression in a non-European context.[15] He acknowledges Jesus' connections with the Jewish community of his day. But these carry no theological significance today for Ariarajah. He feels much closer to the Eastern religions in terms of Christian theology.[16]

Now I do not wish to suggest that Noth and Ariarajah are exactly in the same place on the Jewish question in terms of Christian theology. Noth regarded Judaism as spiritually dead after the coming of Christ. Ariarajah continues to view Judaism as an authentic religion, but of no significant consequence for understanding Christian faith, particularly in a non-European context. But in one sense there exists a similarity. Neither sees the Jewishness of Jesus as theologically significant for the interpretation of his message today. I find this perspective quite troubling. While I strongly support the contextualization of Christian theology in differing cultural settings, understanding the Jewish context of Jesus remains indispensable for an accurate understanding of his basic teachings. This point has been strongly emphasized by scholars such as James Charlesworth and Cardinal Carlo Martini, SJ, the retired Archbishop of Milan, a prominent biblical scholar in his own right.

---

[15] *A Sacred Obligation: Rethinking Christian Faith in Relation to Judaism and the Jewish People: A Statement by the Christian Scholars Group on Christian-Jewish Relation*, 1 September 2002 (Boston: Center for Christian-Jewish Learning, Boston College).

[16] Wesley Ariarajah, *Towards a Fourth Phase in Jewish-Christian Relations: An Asian Perspective*, Unpublished paper, Conference on Christian-Jewish Dialogue Temple Emmanuel, New York, co-sponsored by the Center for Interreligious Understanding and the Office of Interreligious Affairs of the World Council of Churches, November 2003.

Cardinal Martini has written that "Without a sincere feeling for the
Jewish world, and a direct experience of it, one cannot fully understand Christianity. Jesus is fully Jewish, the apostles are Jewish,
and one cannot doubt their attachment to the tradition of their fore-
fathers."[17] And the 1985 Vatican *Notes* on preaching and teaching
about Jews and Judaism declares that "Jesus was and always
remained a Jew ... Jesus is fully a man of his time, and his envi-
ronment — the Jewish Palestinian one of the 1st century, the anx-
ieties and hope of which he shared."[18] Fortunately not all Asian theologians share the Ariarajah's perspective. The prominent
Vietnamese-American scholar Peter Phan has been outspoken in
terms of the Jewish context of Jesus' message. He is in fact one of
the signatories of the statement *A Sacred Obligation*. Scholars such
as Phan, while trying to integrate Christ and his message into Asian
cultural traditions understand that such integration cannot authentically take place without an effort to understand the original message of the New Testament. And such understanding is impossible
without a deep grasp of Jewish religious thought in the time of
Jesus and the period of the New Testament's composition.

Another example of a biblical scholar whose writings helped to
undercut Jesus' ties to Judaism is Rudolf Bultmann. He has exer-
cised a decisive influence over Christian biblical interpretation for
many years. In recent years this influence has begun to wane.
Arthur Droge has spoken of a recent liberation of biblical scholarship from the Bultmannian captivity on the question of Jesus and
Judaism.

[17] Carlo Martini, S.J., "Christianity and Judaism: A Historical and Theological Overview," *Jews and Christians: Exploring the Past, Present, and Future*, ed.
James Charlesworth (New York: Crossroad, 1990) 19.

[18] The Notes may be found in Helga Croner (ed.), *More Stepping Stones to
Jewish-Christian Relations: An Unabridged Collection of Christian Documents
1975-1983* (New York: Paulist, 1985).

For Bultmann a Jewish people cannot be said to exist with the onset of Christianity. In his perspective Jewish religious expression removed God to a distant realm. In contrast, the continued presence of Christ in prayer and worship enabled each individual Christian to come ever closer to God. Again, Bultmann's viewpoint stands contrary to the position of a growing number of contemporary biblical scholars and church documents which depict Jesus and his disciples as profoundly intertwined in their fundamental religious outlook with the Judaism of the time.

There is little question that the dominant exegetical approach during most of the twentieth century continued to sustain the classical covenantal displacement theology with respect to Judaism. It is only in the latter part of the twentieth century and into the present century that scholars such as James Charlesworth, Douglas Hare, Daniel Harrington, Clemens Thomas and Robin Scroggs, to name but a few, have moved New Testament interpretation in directions opposite to that advanced by the likes of Bultmann and Kittel. This new exegesis is gradually forcing theologians to rethink significantly the theology of the Christian-Jewish relationship, redirecting it away from the long dominant supersessionist approach towards an emphasis on a continuing interrelationship rooted in the affirmation of continued Jewish covenantal inclusion after the Christ Event.

One church document that takes this new exegesis as a starting point for its theological reflections on the Christian-Jewish relationship comes from the Leuenberg Church Fellowship, an association of the Reformation churches in Europe. Its 2001 document *Church and Israel*, published both in English and German, argues that the interrelationship between the Church and Israel is not a marginal issue for Christianity. Rather it represents a central dimension of ecclesiology. The relationship with Israel is seen in this document as an indispensable foundation of Christian faith.

The Church is required to reflect on its relationship with Judaism because of its profound linkage to the Jewish community in its beginnings. "The biblical texts referring to these beginnings," according to this document, "do not only speak of the historical origin of the Church and thus of the historical relation with Israel; they also form the starting point and critical point of reference (*fons et iudex*) for all theological reflection."[19]

This recent biblical scholarship coupled with official church teaching is now saying that any portrayal of Jesus that separates him from the Judaism of his time in the manner of Bultmann, Noth or even Ariarajah represents a truncated and distorted presentation of his message and mission. It is ironic that, at least in the case of Ariarajah, he would want to inculturate the gospel by de-inculturating Jesus himself. Certainly it is legitimate to present the image of Jesus through various cultural symbols and images. But Jesus the Jew is not one among manifold ways of presenting Jesus. It forms the base for authentically interpreting his fundamental message. Without maintenance of this fundament efforts to translate the meaning of Jesus' message into a variety of cultures, a quite legitimate and necessary effort as I already said, will likely eviscerate important dimensions of this message.

One of the best summaries of where we are today in terms of Jesus' relationship to the Judaism of his time and the implications it carries for understanding a theology of Christian-Jewish covenantal bonding can be found in the writings of Robin Scroggs.

---

[19] Cf. The Leuenberg Church Fellowship, *Church and Israel: A Contribution from the Reformation Churches in Europe to the Relationship Between Christians and Jews* (Frankfurt am Main: Verlag Otto Lembeck, 2001) 1.3 and 3.1. Also cf. the statement by the discussion group "Jews and Christians" of the Central Committee of German Catholics, "Jews and Christians in Germany: Responsibility in Today's Pluralistic Society," available on the website of the Center for Jewish-Christian Learning at Boston College (http://www.bc.edu/research/cjl).

His view was accepted by the late Cardinal Joseph Bernardin of Chicago, a leader in promoting Jewish-Christian reconciliation.[20]

Scroggs emphasizes the following points: (1) The movement begun by Jesus and continued after his death in Palestine can best be described as a reform movement within Judaism. Little or no evidence exists to suggest a separate sense of identity within the emerging Christian community, (2) Paul understood his mission to the Gentiles as fundamentally a mission out of Judaism which aimed at extending God's original and continuing call to the Jewish people to the Gentiles. (3) Prior to the end of the Jewish war with the Romans in 70 C.E., it is difficult to speak of a separate Christian reality. Followers of Jesus did not seem on the whole to understand themselves as part of a separate religion from Judaism. A distinctive Christian identity only began to develop after the Roman-Jewish war. And (4) the later parts of the New Testament do exhibit the beginnings of a sense of separation between Church and synagogue, but they also retain some sense of continuing contact with the Christian community's original Jewish matrix.[21]

While not every New Testament scholar may subscribe to each and every point made by Scroggs, a consensus is definitely developing that the process of church-synagogue separation was longer and more complex than we once believed. Such a picture significantly challenges how most Christians have understood the situation. They were raised, as I was raised, with the notion that by the time Jesus died on Calvary the church was clearly established as

[20] Robin Scroggs, "The Judaizing of the New Testament," *Chicago Theological Seminary Register* 75 (Winter 1986) 1.

[21] Cf. Wayne Meeks and Robert Wilken, *Jews and Christians in Antioch in the First Four Centuries* (Missoula, MT: Scholars Press, 1978); Robert Wilken, *John Chrysostom and the Jews: Rhetoric and Reality in the Late 4th Century* (Berkeley, CA: University of California Press, 1983). Cf. also Anthony Saldarini, "Jews and Christians in the First Two Centuries: The Changing Paradigm," *Shofar* 10 (1992) 32-43.

a distinct religious body apart from Judaism. This understanding was subsequently expanded, especially by the Church Fathers, into what his known as the *adversos Judaeos* tradition which had as a theological centerpiece the total displacement of the Jewish people from the covenant.[22] But more and more, thanks to such scholars as Robin Scroggs, we are coming to see that many people in the very early days of Christianity did not interpret the significance of the Jesus movement as inaugurating a new, totally separate religious community that would stand over against Judaism.

It does not appear that Jesus conveyed to his disciples and followers a clear sense that he meant to create a new and distinct religious entity called the Church that was to be totally independent of Judaism. This separate identity only emerged gradually well after his death. And we now know through the research of scholars such as Robert Wilken, Wayne Meeks, Alan Segal and Anthony Saldarini that this development was of several centuries duration in a number of areas of the Christian world.[23] Evidence now exists for regular Christian participation in Jewish worship, particularly in the East, during the second and third centuries and, in a few places, until the fourth century.

The challenge now facing Christianity in light of this new research on the origins of the Church is to ask whether the creation of a totally separated religious community was actually in the mind of Jesus himself. This is something that Cardinal Martini has addressed. In some of his writings he has reintroduced the idea of 'schism' into the discussion of the basic theological relationship

[22] Cf. Rosemary Ruether, *Faith and Fratrice: The Theological Roots of Anti-Semitism* (New York: Seabury, 1974). Cf. also David E. Froymson, "The Patristic Connection," *Antisemitism and the Foundations of Christianity*, ed. Alan Davies (New York/ Ramsey/Toronto: Paulist, 1979) 98-117.

[23] Carlo Martini, "The Relation of the Church to the Jewish People," *From the Martin Buber House* 6 (1984) 3-10.

between Jews and Christians, a notion that first appeared in the early part of the twentieth century. Martini applies the term 'schism' to the original separation of the church and synagogue. For him the break between Jews and Christians represents the fundamental schism, far more consequential in negative terms than the two subsequent ruptures within Christianity itself. In introducing the notion of schism, Martini has interjected two important notions into the conversation. For schism is a reality that ideally should not have occurred and which should be seen as a temporary situation rather than a permanent reality. So schism, which had been used previously only in terms of the two inter-Christian separations, implies a certain mandate to heal the rupture that has ensued.

There is legitimate room for debate as to the appropriateness of the term 'schism' in reflecting on the nature of the Christian-Jewish theological relationship today. I myself do not think it will take us too far. But behind it lay the strong conviction on Martini's part that we cannot forge a meaningful theological self-identity within contemporary Christianity without a restoration of the profoundly Jewish context of Jesus' teaching. Clearly the Church will not return to an understanding of itself as one among many Jewish groups. But, in light of recent biblical scholarship, it will need to reassess how its self-identity is rooted in Judaism. This is the challenge that Ariarajah's contention about the inconsequential nature of Judaism for Christian theological self-understanding presents today. Christian theology will have to respond in the coming years to this challenge. Is Ariarajah correct or is someone such as Johann Baptist Metz correct. In a diametrically contrary way Metz has argued that "Christians can form and sufficiently understand their identity only in the face of the Jews."[24] For Metz such a vision

---

[24] Cf. Metz, "Facing the Jews." Cf. also Johann Baptist Metz, *The Emergent Church* (New York: Crossroad, 1981).

involves a definite reintegration of Jewish history and Jewish beliefs into Christian theological consciousness and statement. Jewish history is not merely Christian pre-history. Rather it forms an integral, continuing part of ecclesial history.

As biblical scholars and theologians have begun to probe the implications of this new vision of Jesus as profoundly intertwined with the Jewish community, two initial approaches have emerged in terms of understanding the theological relationship between the Church and the Jewish people in a new way in terms of covenantal inclusion. Within each approach different nuances appear as we move from scholar to scholar. Yet all affirm a central linkage between Judaism and Christianity. We can generally characterize the two trends as 'single covenant' and 'double covenant' with a few scholars calling for an understanding of the Jewish-Christian relationship within a multi-covenant framework.[25]

The 'single covenant' perspective sees Jews and Christians as basically united within one covenantal tradition with its origins at Sinai. This one ongoing covenant was in no way ruptured through the Christ Event. Rather the coming of Christ represented the decisive moment when the Gentiles were able to enter fully into the special relationship with God already enjoyed by Jews, a relationship they continue to maintain. Some scholars opting for this approach argue that the decisive features of the Christ Event do impact all people, including Jews, but not in a way that results in the breaking of already existing Jewish covenantal ties. Others would have the Christian appropriation

[25] Ruether and Paul Knitter are two examples of this perspective. Marcus Braybrooke, in a volume entitled *Christian-Jewish Dialogue: The Next Steps* (London: SCM, 2000), has argued for further reflection on how we might relate Jewish-Christian covenantal thinking to the wider dialogue of world religions. I myself have taken up this important theme as well: Pawlikowski, "Toward a Theology of Religious Diversity," *Journal of Ecumenical Studies* 11 (Winter 1989) 138-153.

and reinterpretation of the original covenantal tradition in and through Jesus apply primarily to non-Jews. This would seem to be the argument that Cardinal Walter Kasper has made in a number of addresses and articles over the past several years. Kasper would argue that Jews represent an altogether special case in the history of salvation from the Christian perspective. This view has also been expressed by Cardinal Kasper's colleague at the Vatican, Archbishop Michael Fitzgerald who heads the office for relations with peoples of other faiths except for the Jews. This is essentially a viewpoint shared by Pope John Paul II as well. One major Protestant theologian who took the single covenantal perspective in his writings was the late Paul van Buren, although towards the end of his career he seemed to be moving back towards a more classical outlook rooted in the thought of his mentor Karl Barth.[26]

I see several problems with the single covenant approach. In the first instance it is highly dependent on a linear understanding of the Jewish-Christian relationship. Even when that linear notion has been expressed in fairly positive terms ('mother-daughter' or 'elder brother-younger brother') it can still mask a certain form of theological fulfillment in Christianity that renders Judaism a second class religion. I fear that such an attitude lies behind Cardinal Avery Dulles' assertion that there are not two independent covenants for Jews and Christians. Dulles insists that Jews are not saved through the Sinai covenant alone but only through the completion of the one covenant through Christ's death and resurrection.[27]

---

[26] Franz Mussner, *Tractate on the Jews: The Significance of Judaism for Christian Faith* (Philadelphia, PA: Fortress, 1984). Cf. also Id., "From Jesus the 'Prophet' to Jesus the 'Son'," *Three Ways to the One God: The Faith Experience in Judaism, Christianity and Islam*, ed. Abdoldjavad J. Falaturi, Jacob J. Petuchowski, and Walter Strolz (New York: Crossroad) 76-85.

[27] Dulles, "Evangelization and the Jews," 10.

The linear thrust of single covenant perspective appears increasingly problematical in light of new scholarship. An increasing number of scholars today, Daniel Boyarin for one, are emphasizing what Boyarin terms the 'co-emergence' of Judaism and Christianity today from within a common religious revolution in Second Temple Judaism. While the parallel understanding would still preserve a common Jewish/Christian core, it tends to stress their distinctive responses to the fundamental covenantal relationship. Such an outlook renders any simple notion of a single covenant, especially in terms of theological fulfillment, increasingly difficult to sustain. Yet I believe that Boyarin and others have made a strong case for their parallel approach.[28]

The 'double covenant' theory begins at more or less the same starting point as its single covenant counterpart. Jews and Christians continue to remain bonded despite their somewhat distinctive appropriation of the original covenantal tradition. But it prefers to highlight the distinctiveness of the two communities and their traditions particularly in terms of their experiences after the final separation of the church and synagogue. I have personally favored this view over the years though it certainly needs qualification.

Christians associated with this perspective insist on maintaining the view that through the ministry, teachings, and person of Jesus a vision of God emerged that was distinctively new in terms of some central features. Even though there may well have been important groundwork laid for this emergence in Second Temple

---

[28] Daniel Boyarin has been working for several years on a "Co-Emergence" Project. Three of his books have amplified this theme: Daniel Boyarin, *Dying for God: Martyrdom and the Making of Christianity and Judaism* (Palo Alto, CA: Stanford University Press, 1999), *A Radical Jew: Paul and the Politics of Identity* (Berkeley, CA: University of California Press, 1997), and *Border Lives: The Partition of Judaeo-Christianity* (Philadelphia, PA: University of Pennsylvania Press, 2005).

or Middle Judaism, what came to be understood regarding the divine-human relationship, and hence ultimately covenantal relationship, through the Christ Event has to be seen as distinctive.[29]

An important example of the double covenant approach can be found in the writings of the German theologian Franz Mussner.[30] Mussner highlights Jesus' deep, positive links to the Jewish tradition of his day. He likewise rejects any interpretation of the Christ Event over against Judaism in terms of Jesus' fulfillment of biblical messianic prophecies. Rather, for Mussner, the uniqueness of the Christ Event arises from the complete identity of the work of Jesus, as well as his words and actions, with the work of God. As a result of the revelatory vision in Christ, the New Testament is able to speak about God with an anthropomorphic boldness not found to the same extent within the biblical or postbiblical tradition of Judaism.

In answer to the question of what the disciples finally experienced through their close association with Jesus, Mussner speaks of "a unity of action extending to the point of congruence of Jesus with God, an unheard of existential imitation of God by Jesus."[31] But this imitation, Mussner insists, is in keeping with Jewish thinking, a contention that many Jewish scholars would certainly challenge, though Elliot Wolfson has argued that the rabbinic corpus

---

[29] On my Christological writings: John Pawlikowski, *Christ in the Light of Christian-Jewish Dialogue* (Eugene, OR: Wipf and Stock, 2001); *Jesus and the Theology of Israel* (Wilmington, DE: Michael Glazier, 1989); "Christology, Anti-Semitism, and Christian-Jewish Bonding," *Reconstructing Christian Theology*, ed. Rebecca Chopp and Mark Lewis Taylor (Minneapolis, MN: Fortress Press, 1994); and "The Christ Event and the Jewish People," *Thinking of Christ: Proclamation, Explanation, Meaning*, ed. Tatha Wiley (New York/London: Continuum, 2003) 103-121.

[30] Mussner, *Tractate on the Jews*, 226.

[31] *Ibid.*

does reveal some evidence of a modified incarnational theology.[32] For Mussner, the uniqueness of Jesus arises from the depth of his imitation of God. So the most distinctive feature of Christianity for Mussner when contrasted with Judaism is the notion of incarnation rather than the fulfillment of messianic prophecies. And even this Christian particularity, he insists, represents an outgrowth of a sensibility profoundly Jewish at its core.

I myself have argued in somewhat the same vein as Mussner. I do believe that the distinctive identity of Christianity vis-à-vis Judaism primarily resides in the notion of the incarnation. And, with Mussner, I see some Jewish roots for this notion in the growing sense of God's proximity to humanity that Ellis Rivkin has argued represents the core of Pharisaism, the Jewish movement which, in the words of the 1985 Vatican *Notes* on Jewish-Christian relations, Jesus stood closest to with regard to a basic religious worldview.

At this point there is need to note another aspect of the ongoing relationship between the Church and the Jewish people within the framework of covenantal theology. Metz has made it and so have I. The consideration of a theology of the covenant cannot be oblivious to the contemporary problem of God, especially in light of the Holocaust. Irving Greenberg, for example, has maintained that the covenant now becomes voluntary in the shadow of Auschwitz. Any covenantal theology must grapple with the issue of what kind of understanding of God can sustain a covenantal theology today. We cannot glibly endorse biblical or classical theological categories in this regard without confronting this central question.[33]

---

[32] Cf. Elliot Wolfson, "Judaism and Incarnation: The Imaginal Body of God," *Christianity in Jewish Terms*, ed. Frymer-Kensky, Novak, Ochs, Sandmel and Signer, 239-254.

[33] Cf. Metz, "Facing the Jews." Cf. also Pawlikowski, "Christology after the Holocaust," *The Myriad Christ*, ed. Terrence Merrigan and Jacques Haers (Leuven/Paris/Sterling, VA: Peeters/Leuven University Press, 2000) 381-397. See also

In recent years it has become evident that neither the single nor double covenantal perspectives adequately address all the important issues, at least from the Christian side. Clearly we cannot forge a new covenantal theology in terms of the Christian-Jewish nexus without explicitly taking up the Christological question. This is certainly behind the affirmation in the ecumenical statement *A Sacred Obligation* referenced earlier in this chapter which underlines that "affirming God's Enduring Covenant with the Jewish people has consequences for Christian understandings of salvation." The accompanying paragraph spells out further the challenge facing the Church regarding Christology:

> Christians meet God's saving power in the person of Jesus Christ and believe that this power is available to all people in him. Christians have therefore taught for centuries that salvation is available only through Jesus Christ. With their recent realization that God's covenant with the Jewish people is eternal, Christians can now recognize in the Jewish tradition the redemptive power of God at work. If Jews, who do not share our faith in Christ, are in a saving covenant with God, then Christians need new ways of understanding the universal significance of Christ.[34]

Now that we have come to understand that the theology which interpreted the Christ Event as the fulfillment of Judaism and the inauguration, in Jesus' own lifetime, of a new religious community to replace the 'old Israel' no longer meets the test of historical accuracy, we need to find new ways on expressing Christological distinctiveness that acknowledges at the same time the ongoing participation of Jews in the salvific covenant.

Irving Greenberg, "Judaism, Christianity and Partnership after the Twentieth Century," *Christianity in Jewish Terms*, ed. Frymer-Kensky, Novak, Ochs, Sandmel and Signer, 25-36.

[34] Cf. *A Sacred Obligation* #6.

Because Christology stands at the very nerve center of Christian faith, re-evaluation of Christological affirmations cannot be undertaken superficially. There is a trend found in some sectors of Christianity, especially among those most open to general interreligious understanding, that the Christ Event is only one of several authentic revelations with no particular universal aspect. Such a starting point is not acceptable to myself nor to many people who have championed a significant rethinking of the Church's theology of the Jewish people such as Cardinal Walter Kasper or the biblical scholars and theologians associated with *A Sacred Obligation*. We must maintain from the Christian side some understanding that the Christ Event carries universal significance.

As I have expressed earlier in this chapter, for me incarnational Christology holds out the best possibility for preserving such universalistic dimensions of the Christ Event while opening up authentic theological space for Judaism (as the late Cardinal Joseph Bernardin of Chicago put it).[35] Cardinal Walter Kasper has insisted in several essays since he assumed the role of President of the *Holy See's Commission for Religious Relations* with the Jews that in any reconsideration of our understanding of Christology as a result of new biblical scholarship and official church documents some understanding of Christ's mission as universal needs to be retained. I support Cardinal Kasper in this affirmation.

An important contribution to the Church's ongoing reinterpretation of the meaning of the Christ Event, in light of its new understanding of covenantal theology, appears in a document issued by the Pontifical Biblical Commission in 2001. The document carries a supportive introduction by Cardinal Joseph Ratzinger under whose jurisdiction the Commission falls. Released without much fanfare, this new document opens up several new

---

[35] See note 29.

possibilities in terms of expressing the significance of the Christ Event while leaving theological space for Judaism.[36]

The Pontifical Biblical Commission document, despite some significant limitations in the way it portrays postbiblical Judaism, makes an important contribution to the development of a new constructive Christological understanding in the context of Jewish covenantal inclusion. Picking up on *Nostra Aetate*'s assertion that Jews remain in the ongoing covenant after the Christ Event, the document includes two statements that are particularly relevant for any discussion of Christology.

The first assertion is that Jewish messianic hopes are not in vain. This is coupled with a recognition that Jewish readings of the Hebrew Scriptures in terms of understanding human redemption represent an authentic interpretation of these texts. Here we have the seeds of what appears to be a recognition of a distinct salvific path for the Jewish people as a theological principle. In this connection Cardinal Kasper has said that "if they *(i.e.,* the Jews) follow their own conscience and believe in God's promises as they understand them in their religious tradition they are in line with God's plan."[37]

The second affirmation within the Pontifical Biblical Commission document with special significance for Christology is that

[36] Cf. The Pontifical Biblical Commission, *The Jewish People and Their Sacred Scriptures in the Christian Bible* (Vatican City: Libreria Editrice Vaticana, 2002). Also cf. Donald Senior, "Rome Has Spoken: A New Catholic Approach to Judaism," *Commonweal* 130 (31 January 2003) 20-23. Joan E. Cook, "The New PBC Document: Continuity, Discontinuity, and the Progression Revisited," Unpublished paper presented to the Annual Meeting of the Catholic Biblical Association, San Francisco, California, 5 August 2003. Also cf. the articles by Mary Boys, Leslie Hoppe, Michael O'Connor, John Pawlikowski and Amy-Jill Levine in *The Bible Today* 41 (May 2003) 141-172.

[37] Walter Kasper, "Christians, Jews and the Thorny Question of Mission," *Origins* 32/28 (19 December 2002) 464.

when the Jewish Messiah appears he will have some of the same traits as Christ. Though this statement is rather oblique in its formulation and probably would not elicit strong applause from Jewish scholars, its importance for covenantal theology lies in the opening it provides for authentic messianic understanding within Judaism that is not totally dependent on Christianity's use of the Christ symbol for such understanding, It likewise retains some sense of a profound link between the two messianic visions, reaffirming the theological bonding between Jews and Christians that Pope John Paul II has made so central in his many writings on the subject.[38]

The Pontifical Biblical Commission document is a study rooted in biblical exegesis, not a work of systematic theology which lies outside of the commission's mandate. Hence the commission did not draw out the full theological implications of the above statements. But these affirmations certainly can provide building blocks for developing such implications. They provide space for exploring whether the Church can speak about the universal significance of the Christ Event in a way that allows for its articulation through religious symbols not directly connected with Christology, such as Jewish religious symbols. This might in fact prove the most fruitful way of developing a Christology that remains open to covenantal pluralism, particularly with respect to the Jews who are acknowledged to have authentic revelation from the Christian theological perspective as Cardinal Walter Kasper has underscored in a number of recent essays.[39]

[38] Cf. Note #11

[39] Cf. Walter Kasper, "The Good Olive Tree," *America* 185 (17 September 2001) 12-14; Id., "Spiritual and Ethical Commitment in Jewish-Christian Dialogue," *From the Martin Buber House* 30 (Summer 2002) 12-20; and Id., "Christians, Jews and the Thorny Question of Mission," 457; 459-467.

Some may say that the above approach is nothing more than the "anonymous Christian" notion put forth by the renowned German theologian Karl Rahner who profoundly shaped the theology of Vatican II. I do not believe this to be the case. It is suggesting rather an understanding that the process of human salvation revealed in the Christ Event goes beyond its articulation within the Church through symbols associated with the Christ Event. Hence Jews, and perhaps some other religious people, do not have to apprehend it directly through Christological symbolism. It suggests that while the salvific reality behind the Christ symbolism is indeed universal, the specific symbolism associated with this salvific reality within the churches may be more limited in scope than the actual reality.

The above perspective, in my judgment, goes considerably beyond what Rahner proposed under the rubric of "anonymous Christian" where the Christ Event remained the dominant religious symbolism. This proposal certainly remains in the realm of a hypothesis. And clearly it is a hypothesis that primarily aims at helping Christians come to a new self-understanding in light of recent biblical scholarship and magisterial pronouncements regarding the Christian-Jewish relationship. This approach would follow the direction suggested by Luke Timothy Johnson.[40] It would be a way of helping Christians think about themselves with reference to Jews, rather than focusing on a theology of Judaism and the Jewish people from the Church's perspective. While, unlike Johnson, I believe both avenues of reflection need to be pursued, he is correct in claiming that a certain priority should be given to Christian self-understanding. It is also true to say, and Christians need to recognize this, that Jews and other religious communities may not feel any necessity for theological confirmation of their faith perspective from the churches.

---

[40] Metz, "Facing the Jews," 27.

Cardinal Joseph Ratzinger has also recently entered this discussion. Besides giving overall approval to the Pontifical Biblical Commission document (though he does not specifically reference the two key passages in the text), he addressed the issue of the covenantal relationship between the Church and the Jewish people from a theological perspective in his own writings. It would appear that he would exempt Jews from the framework presented in *Dominus Iesus*, the controversial document issued by his doctrinal commission. Cardinal Walter Kasper in commenting on the question of Jews and *Dominus Iesus* cites Cardinal Ratzinger's statement that Jews are an altogether special case in terms of their relationship with the Church. Ratzinger describes Judaism as the foundation of Christian faith, a perspective which Kasper takes to mean *Dominus Iesus* is not applicable to the Jews.[41]

According to Cardinal Ratzinger the Jewish community would move to final salvation through obedience to its revealed covenantal tradition. But at the end time, Christ's Second Coming would confirm their ultimate salvation. It is not clear whether Cardinal Ratzinger would require explicit recognition of Christ as the Messiah from Jews as a condition for their salvific confirmation. In my judgment this 'delayed' messianism of the Christ Event in terms of the Jewish people is not as fruitful a starting point for rethinking Christological understanding today as is the direction found in the Pontifical Biblical Commission document. It would be interesting to know whether Cardinal Ratzinger would wish to

---

[41] Cf. Walter Kasper, "The Church and the Jews," *America* 185 (17 September 2001); and Joseph Ratzinger, "The Heritage of Abraham, the Gift of Christmas," *L'Osservatore Romano* (29 December 2000); *Many Religions — One Covenant* (San Francisco, CA: Ignatius Press, 2000); and *God and the World: Believing and Living in our Time* (San Francisco, CA: Ignatius Press, 2002). For a Jewish response, cf. David Berger, "*Dominus Iesus* and the Jews," *America* 185 (17 September 2001) 7-12.

adapt his position in light of the recent Pontifical Biblical Commission document.

We are thus at a very early stage in the process of rethinking Christology and its impact on a theological understanding of covenant in terms of the Christian-Jewish relationship. As Christians, we may never come to a point where our Christological affirmations will lead us into a theology of religious pluralism that squares totally with the basic faith affirmations of Judaism or other world religions. But I believe we have a continuing obligation to pursue this issue since in our globalized world interreligious understanding is not merely confined to the realm of theological ideas but directly impacts people's life together in community. A shift seems to be emerging at present within Christian theology towards a form of double covenant but with continued Jewish-Christian bonding, a shift that has produced strong disagreement from Cardinal Avery Dulles. But church leaders who have spoken to this question such as Cardinals Kasper and Ratzinger need to develop a much fuller synthesis of their perspectives which at the moment represent only fragments of meaning. This also holds true for scholars who have been re-imagining the Christian-Jewish relationship in terms of 'siblings' or 'fraternal twins', images that seem rooted in the more parallel framework suggested by Daniel Boyarin in his co-emergence project.

Thus far I have considered only the first two assertions introduced at the outset of this essay. To round off my discussion, I would now like to focus on the remaining two and add a third. They are the role of the Old Testament or Hebrew Scriptures in forging Christian theological self-identity and the necessity of a Jewish matrix for fully comprehending Christian teaching plus the very controversial issue of Christian mission to the Jews.

Some years ago I became involved in a debate regarding the name Christians ought to use for the first part of our Bible. I felt

Hebrew Scriptures was a more appropriate term than Old Testament. But the name itself is not the key issue. It is rather how we use this biblical resource in terms of Christian theological self-identity. This discussion has gone for more than a decade with no clear resolution.[42] It surfaced again on the Jewish side with the appearance of *Dabru Emet*, the Jewish statement on Christianity, which asserted that Jews and Christians take authority from the same book. This statement occasioned both harsh and more sober criticism from scholars such as Jon Levinson and David Berger. As a result, *A Sacred Obligation* moderated its statement somewhat, saying that "The Bible Both Connects and Separates Jews and Christians" (#5).

Clearly in the past the Hebrew Scriptures were not generally valued very highly as a resource for Christian self-identity. The most extreme anti-Hebrew Scriptures viewpoint was associated with the ancient Christian writer Marcion who urged their total elimination from the Christian version of the Bible. There are some exceptions to this trend, such as in the Calvinist tradition, but not many. Overall Christians used the Hebrew Scriptures as a foil or merely a prelude for the New Testament. There even developed a strong sense that one could find glimpses of Christian revelation, including Christ and Mary, in these books.

While it is not possible to elaborate on this issue in this essay, it must be said that any Christian covenantal theology in terms of the Church's relationship with the Jewish people will need seriously to reconsider the place of the Hebrew Scriptures. Many years ago the

---

[42] Cf. Roger Brooks and John Collins (eds.), *Hebrew Bible or Old Testament?* (Notre Dame, IN: University of Notre Dame Press, 1990). Also cf. *Dabru Emet*, #2 and *A Sacred Obligation* #5. For a critical Jewish response, cf. John Levenson, "How Not to Conduct Jewish-Christian Dialogue," *Commentary* (December 2001) 31-37. It is followed by a spirited exchange of letters. I briefly address this issue in "Jews and Christians: The Contemporary Dialogue," *Quarterly Review* 4 (Winter 1984) 26-28.

late Roy Eckardt, a pioneer in reinterpreting the Christian theological tradition in terms of Judaism, wrote that the covenant forged at Sinai is in principal no less important than the covenant renewed through Jesus Christ.[43] I have always regarded Eckardt as fundamentally correct on this point. The Hebrew Scriptures cannot serve merely as foil or even prelude for Christian self-understanding. They were not that for Jesus for whom they clearly served as a framework for his religious outlook. Whether we would want to regard them as absolutely 'coequal' in defining Christian theological identity is open to discussion. But if Jews remain part of the ongoing covenant after the Christ Event and if they remain bonded with Christians then logically their sacred books, as well as their interpretations of these books, become an undeniable resource for Christian theology. Yet rarely do they serve this function even today.

Reincorporating the Hebrew Scriptures as a primal resource for Christian theology will not come easy because of the history of their use. But it is simplistic to assert that Christians do not really rely on the Hebrew Scriptures because they have used them in quite different ways. Historically that is true. But the historic turnabout within mainline Christianity on the inclusion of Jews in the covenant after the Christ Event that has occurred over the past forty years forces upon Christians a basic re-evaluation of their role in formulating Christian doctrine.

One cautionary note needs to be sounded here. There is some danger that Judaism as a theological resource for Christianity will become solely and exclusively identified with the Hebrew Scriptures. The Judaism of Jesus' time was already postbiblical and we need to come to understand its perspectives if we are accurately to interpret Jesus' teachings. Scholars such as Cardinals Ratzinger and Kasper seem to fall into this trap. We shall have to ask not only

---

[43] Roy Eckardt, *Elder and Younger Brother* (New York: Schocken, 1973) 142.

how the Hebrew Scriptures function as a continuing theological resource for Christianity but how postbiblical Jewish thinking ought to impact on Christian thinking. The 1985 Vatican *Notes* do emphasize the importance of Christians coming to know postbiblical Jewish thought, but seem to imply that this is merely so that we better understand contemporary Judaism. While that is correct, it is also important that we begin to appreciate that, given Jewish-Christian covenantal bonding, present-day Jewish interpretations of Scripture and tradition should impinge not only on overall Christian doctrine but also on specific religious and ethical issues.

Regarding the reincorporation of Christianity into its original Jewish matrix much that has already been said in this essay covers this theme. I would only repeat here a point that we already saw in the writings of Johann Baptist Metz, but this time in the words of Cardinal Walter Kasper: "Christianity therefore cannot be defined without reference to biblical Israel and to Judaism."[44] This means that an understanding of Judaism is integral to an authentic interpretation of Christian doctrine as such, not merely for a theology of Christian-Jewish relations. And as I have underscored in several of my own writings, and as Cardinal Kasper has emphasized as well, Jesus' sense of ethics, ecclesiology and spirituality was profoundly conditioned by his Jewish religious background.[45] There is simply no way to comprehend his vision in these critical areas without a deep grounding in Judaism.

Finally, let me briefly take up the issue of mission. This is certainly one of the most difficult issues in the contemporary Jewish-Christian

[44] Walter Kasper, "Issues Concerning Future Dialogue Between Jews and Christians," Unpublished paper delivered at The Catholic Theological Union, Chicago, 17 April 2002, 3.

[45] See *ibid.*, 10; also cf. Pawlikowski, *Christ in the Light of the Christian-Jewish Dialogue*, 76-107 and Id., "The Jewish Covenant: Its Continuing Challenge for Christian Faith," *The Life of Covenant: The Challenge of Contemporary*

dialogue. The proposed rejection of any notion of mission to the Jews in documents such *A Sacred Obligation* and *Reflections on Covenant and Mission* has encountered strong opposition in sectors of Christianity. The Southern Baptists attacked these documents as well as the Pontifical Biblical Commission document on Jews and the Hebrew Scriptures in the New Testament. Cardinal Avery Dulles took strong exception to *Reflections on Covenant and Mission* on this point.

The issue of mission to the Jews has been a contested issue within Protestantism for sometime. A major Evangelical Christian statement issued from an international conference in Bermuda reiterated a Christian mandate to convert Jews. Within Catholicism where the concrete effort to convert Jews has never been quite as strong as within Protestantism the issue was pretty much kept under wraps since the time of the Council as I emphasized in an address to an international conference held at Cambridge University in 2001.[46] But in the same address I stressed that the issue might surface at any moment within Catholicism. It remained in my view a central, unresolved question in the Christian-Jewish dialogue. A Catholic lay scholar Tomasso Federici spoke to it in a paper delivered at the 1978 Vatican-Jewish International Dialogue held in Venice. In that paper Professor Federici called for the formal termination of any Catholic mission to the Jews on the grounds that the Jews, in light of *Nostra Aetate*, were now recognized as standing within the divine covenantal framework and as possessing authentic revelation from the Christian theological perspective.

Judaism: Essays in Honor of Herman E. Schaalman, ed. Joseph Edelheit (Chicago, IL: Spertus College of Judaica Press, 1986) 113-123.

[46] Pawlikowski, "Maintaining Momentum in a Global Village," *Jews and Christians in Conversation: Crossing Cultures and Generations*, ed. Edward Kessler, John Pawlikowski, and Judith Banks (Cambridge, UK: Orchard Academic, 2002) 75-91.

These same points have been used by Cardinal Kasper to argue as well against any organized effort to convert Jews within Catholicism. Federici's paper was subsequently altered in its final form, to read that "undue" proselytizing of Jews is to be avoided. And Kasper has not further developed his thinking on the matter.[47] *Reflections on Covenant and Mission* represents in fact an effort to develop further the ideas Kasper has put forth on mission to the Jews, something he himself urged in talks at Sacred Heart University and at Boston College.[48]

Certainly there is no easy resolution of the issue of mission to the Jews. Mission has been at the heart of Christian self-understanding. To renounce it for the Jews is to touch the very nerve center of the Christian faith. Some Christians have argued that it represents a failure to love Jews because there is no greater love a Christian can offer anyone than the love made present in the life of Jesus. Certainly we must leave open the possibility of individual conversion in either direction — Jew to Christian or Christian to Jew. But as a theological principle I would support Cardinal Kasper's argument that the Church has no formal obligation to espouse the conversion of the Jews to Christianity through organized missionary efforts. I recognize that this affirmation can open a Pandora's box in terms of mission and other world religions. That is something we need to continue discussing. But for the moment the best we can say is what *A Sacred Obligation* stated in its point #7: "Christians should not target Jews for Conversion." The document then adds that "In view of our conviction that Jews are in an eternal covenant with God, we renounce missionary efforts directed at converting Jews.

---

[47] Tommaso Federici, "Mission and Witness of the Church," *Fifteen Years of Catholic-Jewish Dialogue, 1970-1985,* ed. International Catholic-Jewish Liaison Committee (Rome: Libreria Editrice Vaticana/Libreria Editrice Lateranense, 1988) 46-62.

[48] Cf. Walter Kasper, "Christians, Jews and the Thorny Question of Mission."

At the same time, we welcome opportunities for Jews and Christians to bear witness to their respective experiences of God's saving ways. Neither can properly claim to possess knowledge of God entirely or exclusively."

In light of the above discussion the viewpoint of Gregory Baum cited at the beginning of this essay is definitely confirmed. *Nostra Aetate* in restoring Jews to the divine covenant from a Christian theological perspective opened a radical rethinking of Christian faith identity. Over forty years the major dimensions of this fundamental re-definition have begun to unfold as scholarly research leads to institutional restatement. But clearly a backlash has arisen in some quarters of Christianity.[49] How quickly this process will continue in the coming years, if it continues at all, remains an open question.

---

[49] In a recent article, Cardinal Avery Dulles has questioned whether Vatican II really affirmed the continuity of the Jewish Covenant. I find his claim incomprehensible in light of chapter Four of *Nostra Aetate*, which relies on Paul's affirmation of continuity in Romans 9–11 as well as any number of statements of Pope John Paul II such as Mainz (1980) and the Rome Synagogue address. Dulles again raises up the texts in Hebrews mentioned earlier. In retrospect it would have been good if *Nostra Aetate* had dealt with these texts directly rather than ignoring them. Cf. Avery Dulles, "The Covenant with Israel," *First Things* (November 2005) 16-21.

"THE NEW PEOPLE OF GOD"
A PROTESTANT VIEW

Simon Schoon

The Declaration of the Church to Non-Christian Religions, *Nostra Aetate* # 4 on October 28, 1965, meant a watershed event in the history of relations between the Church and the Jewish people in particular, and between Christians and Jews in general. When we, more than forty years later, recall and commemorate this great event, it gives us the opportunity to look back and to look forwards. Time to consider what needs further reflection, further rethinking, or perhaps asks for a deeper repentance. In this perspective, let me read one sentence from *Nostra Aetate*: "Although the Church is the New People of God, the Jews should not be presented as repudiated or cursed by God, as if such views followed from the Holy Scriptures."

To implement the conciliar Declaration *Nostra Aetate Guidelines and Suggestions* followed in 1974, and *Notes on the Correct Way to Present the Jews and Judaism in Preaching and Catechesis*, in 1985. I will not elaborate on the refining and rewording that took place in the later documents, but will try to give a Protestant reflection on the central theme of the concept "People of God."

Is it possible for the Church to repent as Church, and not only to confess the sinful deeds of some members of the Church? As pope John Paul II prayed in a moving ceremony in St. Peter's Church in Rome on March 12, 2000: "We are deeply saddened by the behavior of those who in the course of history caused these

children of yours [Jews] to suffer." Is it not possible for the Church
to repent as Church? It is not a specific Protestant conviction to
confess that the Church is *Ecclesia semper reformanda*. Was something like that happening in March 2000, when pope John Paul II
approached the Western Wall?

For two thousand years, beginning with the gospels, Christian
theology has depended on the destruction of the Temple as a proof
for the claims that Jesus was the New Temple and the Church was
the New People of God. When the pope devotedly approached the
last vestige of the Second Temple, and when he placed in a crevice
of that wall a piece of paper containing words of his prayer of
March 12, it was more than an apology. The pope created, bend-
ing in prayer at the Western Wall, a new future. The Church was
honoring the Temple it had denigrated. It was affirming the presence of the Jewish people at home in Jerusalem. Does this brave
spiritual deed of the pope require that the confession of *Nostra
Aetate* on the Church as the new People of God should be
changed?

PROTESTANTS: A LOVE-HATE RELATIONSHIP

Before we enter into this question, first a few words on the relations between Protestants and Jews in the past. This relationship is
an emotional one. It shows the ambivalence of a love-hate relationship. On the one hand, Protestants feel because of their love
for the 'Old Testament' a special attachment to the Jews as 'the
people of the old covenant.' On the other hand, they feel resentment,
because this same Jewish people does not accept Jesus as the
promised Messiah. Most Protestants are convinced that the relationship between Christianity and Judaism lies at the very heart of
the Christian faith. Some wholeheartedly choose dialogue, others

remain strong advocates of mission to the Jews. The ambivalence had not yet been overcome in the Protestant-Jewish relationship. This ambivalence comes to the forefront in the discussion on "Who is the (true) People of God?"

The relationship between Protestants and Jews could be characterized as a Love-Hate Relationship. The expression 'love-hate relationship' means that a relation is ambivalent: sometimes the love prevails, sometimes the hate. The one sentiment can easily change to the other and vice-versa. The same expression is used in Dutch, but mentions the hate first, not the love. Perhaps this order: a 'hate-love relationship' would be more adequate, because almost always in history the hatred came first as the strongest feeling, though there were always exceptions. Only the future can show whether the ambivalence in the relationship between Christians can be overcome and the hatred could change into love.

For Protestants the following question is threatening but inescapable: Is theological anti-Judaism a passion that is an inevitable part of Christian identity? Hence follows the question: Is hatred towards Jews ineradicable in Christianity because, one suspects, the aversion to Jews and Judaism originates from the New Testament itself? Is the source of our faith itself poisoned? For Protestants with their strong emphasis on the *Sola Scriptura* principle these questions are perhaps even more painful than for other Christians. The fact cannot be denied that, in the course of church history, expressions of anti-Semitism have been supported in many ways by quotations from the New Testament. In this context the following questions are for us relevant: Does the New Testament speak about the Church as the (New) People of God? And, if so, has this way of speaking about the Church caused and strengthened Christian anti-Semitism?

THE "TRUE PEOPLE OF GOD"

'Israel', 'People of God' and 'Holy People': these are titles the
Church has thought right to assume for itself, at an early point in
its history. In the place of Israel, the Church viewed itself as
elected, called and sanctified by God. So Christian theologians conducted a fierce polemical debate with Jewish scholars on the questions, 'Who is the *true* people?' and 'Whose is the inheritance?'
In other words: who could claim the title of honor 'a kingdom of
priests and a holy nation' (Exod 19:5)? Quite often the struggle
was not decided by words but by brute force. The Church claimed
the exclusive right to the title 'Holy People' and the 'People of
God'. It held that the original Israel had forfeited this right, on
account of its unbelief in the promised and now revealed Savior
Jesus Christ. The Christian aversion toward the Jewish people has
its strongest expression in the long-upheld substitution theory: as
the 'new People of God', the Church has taken over, definitively,
the place of the old Israel as the 'Holy People'.

The Reformers in the 16th century left the substitution theology
unchanged. The 'Holy People' was re-defined as the church of the
Reformation. They emphasized the holiness of those church members who by faith alone were destined to share in the holiness of
Jesus Christ. The Church of the Reformation projected itself retro-
spectively onto the Old Testament, as far back as the Garden of
Eden.[1] The history of the People Israel in the Old Testament age
was annexed ecclesiologically.

---

[1] See for example in Calvinist tradition Question and Answer 54 of the Catechism of Heidelberg: "What do you believe concerning the 'Holy Catholic
Church'? That the Son of God, out of the whole human race, from the beginning
to the end of the world, gathers, defends, and preserves for Himself, by his Spirit
and Word, in the unity of the true faith, a Church chosen to everlasting life; and
that I am, and forever shall remain, a living member thereof."

In the centuries-long struggle where the 'pure church' was to be found, much attention had been given to the four *notae ecclesiae*, the 'notes' of the 'true church': its unity, its holiness, its catholicity and its apostolicity. The Reformation reduced the four *notae* of the Church to only two. These were the pure preaching of the Word and the proper administration of the two sacraments, Baptism and Holy Supper, while some parts of Calvinism added a third *nota*, namely the right application of Church discipline. Little if any thought was given to the connection of the Church to God's ancient people Israel, let alone that this connection could be seen as a *nota ecclesiae*. There was not a single theological acknowledgement of the continuing history of the living Jewish people after the coming of Christ. Only in modern times has this debate on the 'true people' reached the level of a real dialogue, though not yet in all parts of the world, and not in every part of pluralist Protestant Christianity.

In the context of the Jewish-Christian dialogue it has been proposed more than once that churches of every background and denomination should be ready to drop their self-definition of 'the Church as God's (Holy) People', so as to create a new climate in the Jewish-Christian relationship. Considering the enormous diversity of churches and opinions in Christianity, this is probably unattainable and unrealistic in practice. During the Second Vatican Council (1962-1965), the Roman Catholic Church re-discovered the Church as 'the People of God on the way' and favored this title as a proper correction of the existing sacramental and clerical vision of the Church. Also in the theology of the World Council of Churches, founded in 1948, to which the majority of Protestant and Eastern Orthodox Churches belong, the identification of the Church with 'God's People' has become a popular way of speaking.[2] One

---

[2] Allan Brockway, Paul van Buren, Rudolf Rendtorff and Simon Schoon, *The Theology of the Churches and the Jewish People* (Geneva: WCC Publications, 1988).

must wonder, though, whether a renewal of the relationship between Christians and Jews demands such a radical step as giving up the title 'Holy People'. Jewish partners in dialogue do not ask for such 'sacrifices' and make no such demands on the self-definition of Christians, provided this poses no implicit threat to their own self-understanding and existence. From this viewpoint, the theological challenge for Christians is not so much whether to renounce the term 'People of God' for the Church, as to use this term in such a manner that no anti-Jewish responses will result from it.

1 PETER 2:9

The *locus classicus* for the 'Church — as God's people' theology is undoubtedly 1 Pet 2:9. In this oft-quoted text, the Church is crowned with the Old Testament titles of Israel from Exod 19:5-6: "You are a chosen race, a royal priesthood, a holy nation, God's own people." In 1 Pet 2:10, with an allusion to Hos 2:23, the author identifies the Church with God's People. 1 Peter is difficult to date precisely, and could be placed anywhere between 70-100 C.E., written by an unknown writer who stood more or less in the Pauline tradition.[3] Old Testament material plays a very important structural role in 1 Peter.[4] This role is theological: The writer re-reads and re-interprets the authoritative text of the Old Testament from a new perspective, in light of what he regards as the definitive

---

[3] See Norbert Brox, *Der erste Petrusbrief*, Evangelisch-katholischer Kommentar zum Neuen Testament, 21 (Zürich: Benzinger, 1979) 38-51.

[4] Cf. Jo Bailey Wells, *God's Holy People: A Theme in Biblical Theology*, Journal for the Study of the Old Testament. Supplement Series, 305 (Sheffield: Sheffield Academic Press, 2000) 203-246.

revelation of God in Jesus Christ. The text of 1 Pet 2:9-10 is regarded by commentators as the pivot of 1 Peter. In the preceding verses 2:6-8 the "stone," quoted and "lifted" from Ps 118:22, is christologically applied in a totally new context: "Come to him, to that living stone, rejected by men but in God's regard chosen and precious," and those who believe in Jesus Christ are called themselves "living stones ... built into a spiritual house, to be a holy priesthood." The mentioning of the holy priesthood in this verse is already an allusion to Exod 19:6 and leads in 1 Pet 2:9-10 to the more explicit quotation of Exod 19:5-6, in which the titles of Israel seem to be clearly transferred to the Church.[5]

The biblical theologian Wells states: "All the terms and associations of Israel's election, which were initially attributed to Christ, are now applied to the body of believers in their relationship to Christ. So we find expressed here the themes of holiness — the special status, the special character, the special purpose — focused upon the people of God in Christ."[6] The emphasis of the author of 1 Peter, however, is not in the first place ecclesiological; he has a much more ethical and missionary purpose. He wants in his letter to encourage Christians, in their situation of estrangement as "aliens and exiles," to live up to the high standard of their election and calling: "that you may declare the wonderful deeds of Him who called you out of darkness into his marvelous light (1 Pet 2:10)." In this way, the New Testament canon established a new context for reinterpreting the themes of holiness and peoplehood.[7]

---

[5] See for a modern elaboration in the Lutheran tradition of this theme for the ecclesiology and liturgy of the Church: Gordon Lathrop, *Holy People: A Liturgical Ecclesiology* (Minneapolis, MN: Fortress, 1993) especially 207-227.

[6] Wells, *God's Holy People*, 222.

[7] See for the reinterpretation of the Old Testament in the New Testament: Schoon, "De Schrift: basis voor gesprek tussen joden en christenen?," *Joden,*

The conclusion may be that upholding the Church as 'People of God' could not be seen merely as a later development, and therefore as a negative outgrowth of the substitution doctrine, but can refer back to various texts of the New Testament. It has been demonstrated that it is also possible to find different emphases in the New Testament and to put forward different nuances. Though in the New Testament the honorary titles for Israel are only seldom entirely transferred to the Church, this happened on a large scale in church history. That this was also the case in Protestantism will be shown below with a number of classical examples. I have to limit myself and will mention only some examples from my own tradition, the Reformed tradition of Protestantism.

JOHN CALVIN

For Calvin (1509-1564) the Church is chosen by God before the foundation of the world. The holiness of the Church derives from Christ and is effected and preserved in the practical life of the Church by the proclamation of the Word, the administration of the sacraments, and the enforcement of Church discipline.[8] To prove the holiness of the Church, Calvin often refers to 1 Cor 1:30, where Paul writes that the believers are sanctified by Jesus Christ: "He is the source of your life, whom God made our wisdom, our

---

christenen en hun Schrift: Een bundel opstellen aangeboden bij het afscheid van C. J. den Heyer, ed. Chris Houtman and Peerbolte Lietaert (Kampen: Ten Have, 2001) 161-177.

[8] Pieter Johannes Richel, *Het kerkbegrip van Calvijn* (Dissertation, Utrecht, 1942) 189-192. Cf. also Otto Weber, *Grundlagen der Dogmatik*, Band II (Neukirchen: Buchhandlung des Erziehungsvereins, 1962) 609-625.

righteousness and sanctification, and redemption." On the one hand, he dissociates himself from the Roman Catholics, whom he accuses of setting up an ideal of the holiness of the Church in it self, apart from Christ. On the other hand, he turns himself against the Anabaptists, who according to him want to establish a Church without any sin and error, in the tradition of the Donatists and Cathars. Because the holy Church cannot be "to the dishonor of God (...) a conspiracy of wicked and abandoned men," he regards Church discipline as one of the *notae ecclesiae* that serves "like a bridle to restrain and tame those who rage against the doctrine of Christ."[9]

Calvin's struggle for a 'holy Church' and his doctrine of Church discipline must be seen in the context of his time, in which he tried to establish a kind of theocracy in Geneva and saw the Roman Catholic Church as a revelation of the Antichrist. Often the Jews are mentioned and used in the *Institutes* of Calvin to illustrate the terrible failures of the Catholics, whom he refers to as the 'Romanists'. The Jews of the Old Testament serve as a 'model of disobedience' to expose the sins of the 'Romanists' of his time: "The Romanists, therefore, today make no other pretension than what the Jews once apparently claimed when they were reproved for blindness, ungodliness, and idolatry by the Lord's prophets."[10] However, unlike Luther, Calvin was not so harsh in his criticism toward Jews, because he had not much contact with them and they were no serious threat to his reformation in Geneva. There was also a major doctrinal reason: he was con-

---

[9] John Calvin, *Institutes of the Christian Religion* (London: Clarke, 1960) Book IV, Ch. XII on Church Discipline (quotations: IV/XII/1, 5). See for an attempt to modernize the practice of Church discipline: B. Wentsel, *De Heilige Geest, de kerk en de laatste dingen: De kerk als het saamhorige volk Gods*, Dogmatiek deel 4b (Kampen: Kok, 1998) 786-813.

[10] Calvin, *Institutes*, Book IV, Ch. II/3.

vinced of the unity of the Old and New Testament. He emphasized the one covenant, and believed in the continuing use of the law by Christians.[11]

Although Calvin could openly speak about the Church as 'the (holy) People of God', a Church which existed for him already in the time of the Old Testament, yet he preferred the term 'covenant' to the name 'holy Church'. His *Institutes* are built up around this central concept. For him the unity of the one covenant was a very important conviction, a covenant which had started in Old Testament times, and was widened and fulfilled by Jesus Christ. The same salvation which was revealed in its fullness in the New Testament, was already the salvation of the Old Testament, but there it was only present in 'shadows'. The Law of the Old Testament is fulfilled, not finished, in the New Testament, and serves not only as a means to discover sins, but is primarily meant to show believers the way to live according to God's will in thankfulness.

Calvin mentioned the historical dispensations of the one covenant, which relate in his view to God's pedagogical motives in his revelation to Israel and the Church. The essence or substance of the covenant remains the same in the different dispensations, namely the person of Christ.[12] There is not much room in his christological thinking for a dynamic history of the covenant of Israel during the time of the Old Testament and there is no room at all for an active continuation of the covenantal history of Israel after Christ. Except for some remarks in his exegesis of Rom 11 he does not speak about the future of Israel and the Jews. Yet his emphasis on the one and only covenant and his extensive attention to the Old Testament has given later Calvinist tradition many points of

[11] Cf. Jack Robinson, *John Calvin and the Jews* (New York: Peter Lang, 1992).

[12] Calvin, *Institutes*, Book II, Ch. X/4.

contact to elaborate on the theological significance of the Jewish
people.[13]

KARL BARTH

Many Protestants regard the Swiss theologian Karl Barth (1886-
1968) as the 'church-father' of the 20th century. He wrote exten-
sively on the Jewish people in his *Church Dogmatics*. As a
Reformed theologian — in line with the Reformer Calvin — he
took his starting point in the concept of the one covenant. He
regarded this covenant, which God had begun with the people
Israel, as the basis of God's plan to reach the whole world. By the
universalization of this covenant through the event of Jesus Christ,
the Church became the real partner of the original covenant. The
fulfillment of the covenant in Christ was already meant as its deepest intention during the period of the Old Testament. It is Barth's
conviction that the covenant of God with Israel had never been
abrogated, though it was undoubtedly fulfilled and confirmed in
Jesus Christ. This christological fulfillment is regarded as the antici-
pation of the coming Kingdom of God.

Yet, in the theology of Barth many remnants of the anti-Jewish
'teaching of contempt' of the Christian Church can be found. On
the one hand, he introduced a much more dynamic concept of
covenant than was common in Christian theology at that time and
emphasized strongly the significance of biblical Israel as a people
of God. On the other hand, he could not — by the very Christological concentration of his theological project — give genuine

---

[13] See Hans-Joachim Kraus, "'Israel' in der Theologie Calvins: Anstöße zu
neuer Begegnung mit dem Alten Testament und dem Judentum," *Kirche und
Israel* (1989) 3-13.

room to the living continuation of the covenant history of the Jewish people after the destruction of Jerusalem and the Temple in the year 70.[14] He regarded Israel as the "natural context of Jesus Christ."[15] So he recognized theologically the concrete 'Israel after the flesh', but only in the light of Jesus Christ. He spoke about Israel and the Church as the two figures of the one Community of God in the world, but because of the rejection of Jesus by the synagogue Israel is called by Barth "the witness of God's wrath" and "the mirror of God's judgment." In contrast, the Church is described as "the witness of God's grace."[16] After the crucifixion of Christ the history of Israel should not have been continued in Barth's opinion, and when it was, it can only be seen by him as "unfruitful," "ghostly" and "lacking the true prophecy."[17] At the consummation of history, the synagogue will find its fulfillment when it will be integrated into the Church.

When Barth speaks about the Church as 'people of God', he speaks about the present; when he calls Israel the 'people of God', he speaks about the past. For him the Church is 'holy' because God has set it apart, decisively, from the surrounding world as a being with its own distinct origin, nature, law, and direction. The holiness of the Church is the reflection of its 'Head' Jesus Christ. According to Barth, Christians cannot believe in the Church as they believe in God, because the creed says *credo ecclesiam* and not *credo in ecclesiam*.[18] As long as the Christian community lives in the world,

---

[14] Karl Barth, *Die Kirchliche Dogmatik*, IV/3, 74-78.

[15] *Ibid.*, II/2, 216.

[16] *Ibid.*, II/2, 286-287.

[17] *Ibid.*, IV/3, 76. Cf. also Friedrich-Wilhelm Marquardt, *Die Entdeckung des Judentums für die christliche Theologie: Israel im Denken Karl Barths* (München: Kaiser, 1967) 266-345.

[18] *Ibid.*, IV/1, 765-783. See also on "the community of the saints:" *ibid.*, IV/2, 747-765.

its invisibility is hidden by its visibility. The Church is guilty of failure and error, but it rests on the power of Christ's promise and cannot therefore perish. In the final volume of his *Church Dogmatics* he deals with "The People of God in the World" and compares the present position of the Church as the "people of God" with the experiences of Israel as the "People of God" in the time of the Old Testament.[19] Unlike his friend and pupil the Dutch theologian Miskotte he did not show any interest in living Judaism and rarely engaged in a real dialogue with Jewish thinkers.

PAUL VAN BUREN

In recent decades, some Protestant theologians have explored new theological paths in their approach to the complicated and delicate questions around the themes of 'Holy People', 'People of God', 'People Israel' and 'the Church as People of God'. I will mention two of them in this context: The American theologian Paul M. van Buren (1924-1996), and the German theologian, Friedrich-Wilhelm Marquardt (1928-2002).

In Van Buren's view, the Church is not 'the People of God', which is the title of Israel, but 'the Church of God from the nations'. When he writes on the 'Holy Peoplehood' of Israel, he emphasizes that Israel is witness to the total claim of God upon the total life of the whole Jewish people.[20] Therefore, he warns of the danger of secularization in the State of Israel, because Israel should

---

[19] Barth, *Die Kirchliche Dogmatik*, IV/3, 780-872 (on Israel in the Old Testament, 788-792, 830-831, 835-838).

[20] Paul M. van Buren, *A Theology of the Jewish-Christian Reality. 2: A Christian Theology of the People Israel* (New York: Seabury Press, 1983) 159-166.

never become a nation like all other nations. Although, according to Van Buren, the empirical evidence in Israel will always be ambiguous, it is a theological judgment that Israel has to live up to the Torah-standard set by its election. Of course, Van Buren realizes that it could be dangerous for a Christian theologian to define the calling of Israel, but for him this is a consequence of his theology.[21] The Gentile Church has not realized its reliance on Israel, when it has called itself "the People of God" and "Holy People." There is in Van Buren's opinion not "the Church *of* England" or "the Church *of* Sweden," expressions he regards as "remnants of the distortions of 'Christendom'," but only a church *in* England and a church *in* Sweden, or in any other nation. He sees Jesus as "Israel-for-the-Gentiles," only through Jesus, the Jew, does the Gentile Church know the God of Israel.[22] Therefore it is an "incredible idea," that the Gentile Church should try to reach the Jewish people with its Gentile mission, by setting up the incoherent phenomenon of a special "mission to the Jews."[23] From a strictly orthodox Protestant and Reformed standpoint, Van Buren's approach is, of course, labeled as "liberal reductionism,"[24] but in his own view it is theologically the only radical way-out after almost 2000 years of an anti-Jewish Church and theology, the beginning of a reconciliation between the "Church of God" and the "Israel of God."[25]

---

[21] This danger is pointed out in: Stephen Haynes, *Reluctant Witnesses: Jews and the Christian Imagination* (Louisville, KY: Westminster John Knox Press, 1995) 120-140.

[22] Van Buren, *A Christian Theology of the People Israel*, 259-264.

[23] *Ibid.*, 324-328.

[24] Scott Bader-Saye, *Church and Israel after Christendom: The Politics of Election* (Boulder, CO/Oxford: Westview Press, 1999) 77-80.

[25] Paul M. van Buren, *A Theology of the Jewish-Christian Reality. 3: Christ in Context* (New York: Seabury Press, 1988) 102-106.

FRIEDRICH-WILHELM MARQUARDT

The German theologian Marquardt has chosen a new and provocative path in trying to work for and describe a new relationship between the Church and the Jewish people. He realized that Christian theology after Auschwitz could not simply go on as if nothing has happened. It also could not continue by tinkering with cosmetic changes in its doctrines. Only a revolution in Christian theology could, in his view, be an honest response to the abyss of Auschwitz. Never again should Christians make Israel the object of their theology. Jews can speak as subjects for themselves and should not be made mute in Christian theology. Christian theological reflection must be characterized by a radical *Umkehr* ("turn," "repentance").[26] This can only be realized in a living dialogue with Jews. After Auschwitz the many burning questions must remain open, even the question whether God lives. Only God himself can respond to this question in the *eschaton*, "if He wants and lives." Christians can not give up their theological and philosophical reflection on God, because only in this way can they find and describe their identity in relation to the People of Israel.[27]

Marquardt does not write much on the doctrine of the Church in his extensive volumes on systematic theology.[28] He prefers a low-profile ecclesiology in contrast with the ecclesiastical triumphalism of the past. Although the Church is founded on Israel, it has become a Church of the Gentiles. The Church is sent to the

[26] Friedrich-Wilhelm Marquardt, *Vom Elend und Heimsuchung der Theologie: Prologomena zur Dogmatik* (München: Kaiser, 1988) 74-150.

[27] Friedrich-Wilhelm Marquardt, *Eia, wärn wir da — eine theologische Utopie* (München: Kaiser, 1997) 426-430.

[28] Friedrich-Wilhelm Marquardt, *Was dürfen wir hoffen, wenn wir hoffen dürften? Eine Eschatologie*, Band 2 (Gütersloh: Mohn, 1994) 155-164; and Band 3 (Gütersloh: Mohn, 1996) 468-488.

nations, but should never forget that its way began in Jerusalem and is meant to lead back to Jerusalem. The Church is called to be the representative of God and of His people Israel in the world of the nations. It does not replace Israel amongst the nations, because Israel can speak for itself. But the Church has the role of expressing before the nations the "anti-pagan witness of God" in confrontation with the idols and powers of the world (here he uses the wording of the Dutch theologian Miskotte). Its task is not to boast of its high titles, like "People of God" or "Holy People," but to keep and to preach and to practice God's Word in the world. So Marquardt can describe the Church with a metaphor, derived from the exodus-story of Israel. He discovers the Church in a not so flattering image, in "the riff-raff" (in Hebrew: *èrev rav*), the crowd of hangers-on that is following Israel out of the slavery of Egypt on its way to the promised land (Exod 12:38).[29] In a more friendly image he describes the Church as "maker of hymns," for him a beloved way to express the essence of the Church.[30]

CONCLUSIONS

In the last part of this article we seek to answer the following questions: What does it mean for Christian theology to confess that the Jewish people remains 'God's People?' Should Christians give only Israel or only the Church the title 'Holy People' or 'People of God?' Or should they rather affirm that both Israel and the Church

---

[29] Marquardt, *Eine Eschatologie*, Band 2, 160-164. Martin Buber and Franz Rosenzweig, *Die fünf Bücher der Weisung* (Heidelberg, 1976) 184, translate Exod 12:38 as follows: "Auch wanderte vieles Schwarmgemeng mit ihnen hinauf."

[30] Marquardt, *Eia, wärn wir da*, 283.

may appropriate the title 'Holy People' in their own way? Concluding, I would like to defend the thesis that the essence of the Church should not only be expressed by mentioning the four classical *notae ecclesiae*, but that a new *nota* should be added, calling the rootedness of the Church in Israel also a *nota ecclesiae*. I will consider three possible answers and make my own choice clear.

Only Israel the 'People of God'?

Some Christian scholars, like Van Buren and Marquardt, have drawn the theological consequence from their encounter with the Jewish people and Judaism by calling only Israel the 'People of God'. They are convinced that if Christians read the Hebrew Bible in the first place as the Book of Israel, they have to take the self-definition of the Jewish people seriously. They have to accept that the term 'People of God' cannot be deduced from a general and already known 'Gentile' or philosophical concept 'people', consequently applied to the special case of Israel. The Hebrew name for 'Holy People' (*am* or *goj qadosj*), is actually untranslatable and its meaning can only be outlined and explained in approximate theological terms. Theologians like Van Buren and Marquardt speak of Israel as the 'People of God', next to the 'Church of Christ'. This position does justice to Jewish self-understanding but not to Christian self-understanding.

In the 20th century the Church has re-discovered Israel as 'God's Chosen People'. This was formulated in many official statements and messages. The theological consequences of this change of paradigm must still be drawn. In my opinion, the Church should read the Hebrew Bible first as the Book of Israel and secondly as the 'Old Testament', *i.e.* as Book of the Church. Both ways of reading must be accepted as theologically valid for Christians. The Church should listen to the self-understanding of the Jewish people.

According to Jewish religious conviction the election of Israel to be God's People is not a matter of an idea, but a phenomenon in history, connected to the concrete corporeal reality of the Jewish people, as the "Body of Faith."[31] Every trace of gnosticism and spiritualizing is excluded from this reality. The origin of this community is not 'natural', but the outcome off God's goodness and election that is only realized in the physicality and concrete history of the People Israel. Giving up the names 'People Israel' and 'God's People' would mean for the Jewish people full assimilation in the world of the nations and therefore the discontinuation of Jewish identity.

Only the Church the 'People of God'?

For theologians like Calvin and many others it was absolutely clear that the Church had replaced the People of Israel as Gods elected people and that the Church was the *only* legal heir of the title 'People of God'. It has become clear in this article that I reject this position. It is not necessary and certainly not helpful to call the Church 'Israel', even not when it is sometimes explicitly emphasized that this choice of name is not meant to "expropriate the identity of Israel" as Church, but only to "appropriate the identity of Israel."[32] Why should the Church appropriate the name 'Israel', if the New Testament does not do so? Why this insistence after such a long anti-Jewish and anti-Semitic *Wirkungsgeschichte* of

---

[31] Cf. the Jewish author Michael Wyschogrod, *The Body of Faith: God in the People Israel* (San Francisco, CA: Harper & Row, 1989) 175-177.

[32] So George Lindbeck, "Postmodern Hermeneutics and Jewish-Christian Dialogue," *Christianity in Jewish Terms*, ed. Tikva Krymer-Kensky; Radical Traditions (Boulder, CO/Oxford: Westview Press, 2000) 106-113, 357-366; for example: "Losing the image of the church as Israel destroys the self-image of the church as a community chosen by God" (109).

the use of this title for the Church?[33] There are many other images and metaphors for the Church, which clarify the essence of the Church perhaps even better than the term 'People of God', for example the biblical metaphor 'body of Christ'(cf. 1 Cor 12:12-26) and names like 'children of God' (cf. Rom 8:16) and 'new creation' (cf. 2 Cor 5:17).[34]

Both Israel and the Church 'People of God'

In the beginning of this article, the question was asked: Should churches be ready to drop their self-definition as 'the Church as God's People'? Would such a move be helpful in the context of Jewish-Christian dialogue to overcome the centuries-long love-hate relationship between Christians and Jews? Or does the use of this concept for the Church in the New Testament and the long tradition of Christianity make such a radical change impossible? There is in my opinion no need to try to stop the Christian use of this concept, as long as it is not combined with anti-Jewish and anti-Semitic doctrine and rhetoric. It is not easy to erase all remnants of anti-Judaism from the Christian doctrine on the Church, which is shown, for example, in the dogmatic volumes of Karl Barth, where Israel is called "the witness of God's wrath" and "the mirror of God's judgment." In the classical conception, which still exists, the People Israel only in the time of the Old Testament have the role of 'foreshadowing' the coming of the 'Holy Church' in the time of the

[33] In the volume of Jewish and Christian contributors *"Christianity in Jewish Terms"* only the Jewish author Irving Greenberg shows some sympathy for this idea, all the others reject it out of hand: Irving Greenberg, "Judaism and Christianity Covenants of Redemption," *Christianity in Jewish Terms*, 158.

[34] Cf. the South Indian theologian Israel Selvanayagam, "People of God and Peoples of God: Christian Discussions," *People of God, Peoples of God: A Jewish-Christian Conversation in Asia*, ed. Hans Ucko (Geneva: WCC Publications 1996) 67-81.

fulfillment in Christ. However, in a very different context, for example, in the practice of many churches in the Third World, the concept 'People of God' can be used as a liberating term for the poor and oppressed, without any anti-Jewish connotation.

The best option would be in my opinion, to speak of Israel as the first-chosen People of God and of the Church as the also-chosen ecumenical People of God from all the Nations (so Bertold Klappert[35]). The Dutch-Reformed theologian Berkhof calls the church the "firstborn" and "forerunner" of the Kingdom of God, names which he also applies to the People of Israel.[36] The American-Lutheran theologian Stanley Hauerwas has a special preference for the term "resident aliens" to refer to the diaspora-existence of the Church in postmodern times, borrowed from Israel in the Old Testament but also used for the Church in 1 Peter, a term with which he wants to mark a radical break with the age-long triumphalism of church history.[37]

Why should we not choose a name the New Testament used for the first followers of Jesus: 'people of the Way' (Acts 9:2; 19:9,23; 22:4; 24:14)? Perhaps there is a feeling that this name is too pretentious after the practice of almost 2000 years of Christianity? Then one could opt for the modest metaphor for the Church, chosen by Marquardt from Exod 12:38, when he compares the Church with the 'mixed multitude' (èrev rav) that follows Israel in the desert out of the house of slavery on its way to freedom.

The conclusion could be that the Church may be called *also* — as one of many different names and metaphors — 'People of

[35] Bertold Klappert, *Miterben der Verheißung: Beiträge zum jüdisch-christlichen Dialog* (Neukirchen-Vluyn: Neukirchener Verlag, 2000) 390-430.

[36] Hendrikus Berkhof, *Christelijk Geloof* (Nijkerk: Callenbach, [7]1993) 402-413.

[37] Stanley Hauerwas and William Willimon, *Resident Aliens: A Provocative Christian Assessment of Culture and Ministry for People who Know that Something is Wrong* (Nashville, TN: Abingdon Press, 1989).

God', when the Church is ready to acknowledge that it is not the first and not the only one to be chosen as God's People. When the Church is ready as Church to repent! The Church is not *the* People of God, but *a* People of God, as is mentioned in Acts 15:14: "God first visited the Gentiles, to take out of them a people for his name." The Church as *ekklesia* represents the eschatological people of God as they are gathered in worship and as they witness to the hope for the coming kingdom of God.

Nota ecclesiae

In my dissertation in 1982, I proposed to call the "rootedness of the Church in (the People of) Israel" one of the *notae ecclesiae*.[38] This is not a totally new attempt, because several theologians have tried to add new *notae* to the four classical *notae ecclesiae*.[39] I would like to confirm and to qualify my earlier position by stating that Christian theology has to develop and to reformulate its Christology and ecclesiology on the basis of the criterion: "Salvation comes from the Jews (John 4:22)." Or, in the words of the apostle Paul to the Gentile Christians in Rome: "Remember it is not you that support the root, but the root that supports you (Rom 11:18)." From the side of the Church there should be a clear confession of solidarity towards the Jewish people, which is grounded in God's election, a solidarity that does not exclude others. This relation of solidarity

---

[38] Simon Schoon, *Christelijke presentie in de Joodse Staat: Theologische overwegingen betreffende de verhouding kerk en Israel naar aanleiding van enkele vormen van christelijke presentie in de staat Israel* (Kampen: Kok, 1982) 253.

[39] John Calvin is already mentioned. More recently: Berkhof, *Christelijk Geloof*, 398-413; Jurgen Moltmann, *Kirche in der Kraft des Geistes: Ein Beitrag zur messianischen Ekklesiologie* (München: Kaiser, 1975) 363-388.

between Christians and Jews will always include an irreducible element of dispute and even rivalry, because of the fact that the 'joint heirs of the promises' interpret these promises of God differently. Both communities call themselves 'holy' in their self-definition and both regard themselves called to be 'holy' by God. In the Protestant view, the 'holy Church' is holy when it is a Church of *metanoia*, of repentance, because the Church must be *semper reformanda*, 'always reforming'. After a long and dreadful history, the Church and the Jewish people could perhaps, on their different ways to the kingdom of God, join forces in a competition for holiness to work for the restoration of the world, separately and together.

Prospects

It is difficult to write anything on the prospects for the future of the relations between the Church and the Jewish people. It cannot be foreseen, whether the change in theological thinking that started because of the shock of the *Shoah*, will be continued in the 21st century, when the living memories of that event will slowly fade and become part of history. Only the future will reveal, whether Judaism will be respected by Church and theology as a living tradition, and whether the theological significance of the existence of the Jewish people will be recognized. This would need a paradigm shift in Church and theology. There are only a few signs that point at this direction, but these signs are still weak and hesitant.

There is not much reciprocity in the dialogue, because interest on the Jewish side remains slight,[40] and on the Christian side the

---

[40] There is no Dutch equivalent of this groundbreaking publication in the United States: Frymer-Kensky, *et al.*, *Christianity in Jewish Terms*. See also David Sandmel, Rosann Catalano and Christopher Leighton (eds.), *Irreconcilable*

ambivalence is still strong. There is the danger of the extremes in the love-hate relationship of Christians towards Jews. Often there is too much love and too much hatred. Jews are regarded as 'devils' or as 'angels'. In the past they were quite often seen in God's design as the 'devils', as the prime movers of history but in the wrong direction. In the present time Jews are sometimes viewed as 'angels', as the main 'players' on the platform of history and therefore responsible for the final coming of the kingdom of God. Both positions are myths and are very dangerous for the existing Jewish people. Jews are in neither extreme accepted as they view themselves, but only as serving Christian aims and as executors of Christian eschatological expectations. All Christian systematic theological thinking on Israel and Judaism can become risky and sometimes even life threatening for Jews.[41]

The great challenge lies in taking up the question whether Church and theology after Auschwitz are capable of overcoming the ambivalence that often has turned into hatred towards Jews and the Jewish people, and whether Christians can learn to live with the duality of kinship and distinction. Many scholars tend to overemphasize the 'back to the roots' concept. This could turn out to be a superficial slogan and runs the risk of serving fundamentalist goals. The New Testament situation in all its diversity cannot be revived and reintroduced. A history of almost 2000 years has left its marks on the present situation. Hermeneutical choices are therefore unavoidable. When the subject of Jews and Judaism comes up in the teaching and preaching of the church, difficult hermeneutical choices will have to be made continuously.

Differences? A Learning Resource for Jews and Christians (Boulder, CO/Oxford: Westview Press, 2001).

[41] See Haynes, *Reluctant Witnesses*.

Perhaps the most important challenge for churches and Christians is to start a new practice in relation to Jews in general and in the Jewish-Christian dialogue in particular, as it is, for example, lived in the Christian project *Nes Ammim* in Israel. This project was started in 1960 by some Dutch and Swiss Christians to turn a new page in the book of Christian-Jewish relations.[42] In the present time it facilitates also peace-work for Jews and Palestinians and offers them a place to meet together. But it is, like some other projects of dialogue and reconciliation, a very small sign of renewal. There is still a long way to go before Christians and Jews will have developed an adult and fruitful relationship of dialogue and reciprocal respect.

---

[42] Schoon and Heinz Kremers, *Nes Ammim: Ein christliches Experiment in Israel* (Neukirchen-Vluyn: Neukirchener, 1978).

NOSTRA AETATE: PAST, PRESENT, FUTURE
A JEWISH PERSPECTIVE

David MEYER

More than forty years after its publication *Nostra Aetate* has lost nothing of its importance. In this chapter I set out to define where we now stand in the dialogue between the Church and Judaism. Since *Nostra Aetate* is the result of development and consultation from within the Church, it is slightly more unusual to reflect on this document from a Jewish perspective. This is however what I propose to do, to put forward a Jewish point of view, to explain how this document is seen from within the Jewish tradition.

To say that the document *Nostra Aetate* — and particular paragraph four of that document — is important, is to do it less than justice. The word 'important' is not strong enough to describe the reality of that which is represented by the ideas expressed in *Nostra Aetate*. It would seem more accurate to use the word 'revolutionary', because the sentiments expressed in this document are indeed a revolution in the state of relations between the Church and Judaism. The word 'revolution' is a powerful word that refers to a radical change in thinking. We all need to accept and to acknowledge the reality of this absolute change, which has truly taken place within the Church in the last forty years.

I would like to add a somewhat more personal note to this initial observation. As someone born in 1967, that is to say two years after the publication of *Nostra Aetate*, I must confess that for me the relations between Judaism and the Church are natural and have always been cordial and respectful. The Church, as I have known it, has never been particularly hostile to Judaism. As a rabbi I have always had numerous contacts with my colleagues in the Churches of the different currents of Christianity or Catholicism. It was only when I began to understand and to study the text of *Nostra Aetate* that I was able to gain some inkling of what the relations between the Church and Judaism must have been like before this document was published. This short and personal analysis shows us very clearly the extensive and positive impact that this document has had on the reality of the dialogue between our two religions.

A final introductory word on the structure of this brief contribution. A chronological approach to the past, present and future of the *Nostra Aetate* declaration, could very well have been a way to reflect on the text under consideration. Yet, this is not the approach I follow. Instead, I will try to look at this document as it was published more than forty years ago, and attempt to find within it, factors that we can use in our thinking about the future relations between the Church and Judaism. To do this, we need to turn around and consider the 'spirit' that animated the creation of this document and that enabled its authors to be genuinely inspired by a commitment to revolution and renewal.

I will focus in particular on four aspects of this document that seem to merit attention. To begin with, the 'spirit' of this document. In what spirit was it created? What were its authors' intentions? What was the atmosphere in which this document was created and written? Secondly, the 'language'. The words used, what do they teach us? How can the words help us think about the real nature of this document and its future? Thirdly, the 'theological aspect'. Clearly, we need to think about the theological reality of a text. What is hidden within it? What theology is reflected in it? What can we learn from it? And finally, fourthly, 'the silences'. Quite simply, let us consider what is missing, what has been left out of this document, which can sometimes reveal, for good and ill, the lacunae in human thinking. 'Lacks' and 'lacunae', or even 'silences' which can push all of us to reach beyond this text, that it is, today, perhaps not sufficient to govern and promote the continuity of relations between the Church and the Jewish people.

Let us begin with 'the spirit'. I have chosen a simple word to describe the spirit that animated the writers of this text: the word 'courage'. Indeed, it must be recognised, that from the point of view of the Church this document is extremely courageous, for it ushers a revolution and a new way of thinking in the Church's doctrine on other religions and on Judaism in particular. The word 'courage', could reflect two different sorts of courage. First, the courage to confront a situation, in other words the courage to question oneself. Then, the courage to change and to develop.

The courage to confront a situation, as this document, *Nostra Aetate*, is the product of the particular atmosphere in the aftermath of the Shoah, the Holocaust, during the Second World War. It is often said and it needs repeating: "not all Christians were Nazis but all the Nazis were children of the Church." This brutal and hard to acknowledge reality made the Church to reflect on its responsibilities in the events that befell the Jewish people during the Nazi period. The Church was not Nazi. There is no doubt on that point. But nevertheless, it was in Christian soil that Nazism took root. And this must lead the Church to reflect on its share of responsibility in that terrible tragedy and in particular with regard to the "teaching of contempt" which for many long centuries was one of the pillars of the catechism in churches.[1]

In the 'spirit' in which *Nostra Aetate* was written, there was first of all the Church's courage in confronting this situation and accepting that its teachings on Judaism were to some degree to blame for what the Nazis did to the Jewish people. This is a courage that few

---

[1] See Jacob Kaplan, *Un enseignement de l'Estime* (Paris: Éditions Stock, 1982, [1]1938).

people possess. It is a courage which still deserves our admiration, for it was certainly not easy for the Church to accept this portion of responsibility. In addition, courage does not end with accepting one's share of responsibility. One also needs to change one's own teachings.

And that is the second form of courage that the text of *Nostra Aetate* shows us. The courage to rethink one's own tradition. Referring ourselves to some Jewish teachings, it would seem relevant to use the expression: "an act of Teshuva,"[2] an act of contrition by the Church. The Church was then ready to look at itself in a mirror, to accept its responsibilities in the "teaching of contempt"[3] and finally to question its teachings and to start teaching on Judaism, the Jews and the Jewish tradition from a different perspective; it is what came subsequently to be called "transforming the teaching of contempt into the teaching of esteem."[4]

What was radical for the Church in this change was that it implied a proper recognition that religion is not only a doctrine that governs relations between man and God. True religion also seeks to govern and to improve the relations between men; the relations between man and man, between individuals. In so doing, the Church was able to turn a corner, to make a step towards change, to think again about this aspect of its own teachings. The Church was capable of rethinking what a religion should be and to reform the bases of the dialogue between people. It seems that this type of

---

[2] "Teshuvah," in Hebrew referring to the need to repent and return on ourselves in order to change our behaviours and teachings. The concept of Teshuvah is at the centre of the festivals of Rosh Hashanah ands Yom Kippur. The word "Teshuvah" comes from the Hebrew root "SHuV" meaning to turn and return.

[3] Jules Isaac (1877-1973), *L'Enseignement du mépris — suivi de L'antisémitisme a-t-il des racines chrétiennes?* (Paris: Éditions Grasset, 2004, reprinted).

[4] Kaplan, *Un enseignement de l'estime.*

courage is a courage that we only encounter when we reach an absolute moral turning point. Clearly, that was the post-war reality for religions and for Christianity in particular. The massacre, on European soil, of six million Jews, including one and a half million children, was possible because of the long centuries of teaching of contempt and anti-Semitic hatred. Faced with this moral turning point, when all dogmas are in doubt and nothing is unthinkable, the leaders of the Church and above all the pope had the courage to rethink and to question everything.

It appears that more than forty years later, this courage to rethink, to revolutionise the dialogue between the religions and between the Church and Judaism in particular, is no longer quite as apparent as it was at that time. In our own days, we all know, the relations between the Church and Judaism are essentially confined to the 'establishment'; to a certain number of privileged individuals or specific structures. Unfortunately, over time this dialogue has become somewhat etiolated and only rarely do we find a freedom of thought, a freedom of reflection and a freedom of courage such as that the authors behind the document of *Nostra Aetate* were able to experience in the flesh and in the spirit. Yet nevertheless, today too, if we want to see a real, continuing and fruitful dialogue between our two religions, it is precisely that same courage, that same flexibility of mind and that same readiness to rethink everything, which we should try to recreate, so as not to lose the advances from those radical changes in the Church's thinking that took place forty years ago.

At this point, let us simply recall that while this liveliness of reflection and courage, is perhaps not altogether in the forefront of relations between Judaism and Christianity today, it would seem that similar qualities could be of benefit to other religions in the world, which seem to find it particularly difficult to enter into relations with and show respect for others. Obviously, I am thinking of Islam, which perhaps could gain something from this form of courage. Just as the Church was capable of rethinking its theology, perhaps the Imams and Islamic leaders could also find in this document a source of inspiration which would help them towards a rethink, towards the possibility of their own religion's 'teaching of esteem' for other religions. In this respect, if we briefly deviate from the strict limits of the Judaeo-Christian dialogue, the text of *Nostra Aetate* remains entirely modern and should be a significant source of inspiration to many of today's religious leaders.

Let us now turn to the second aspect of this paper: 'language', the language used in the writing of *Nostra Aetate*. It must be acknowledged that the language of *Nostra Aetate* is difficult, in particular for a Jewish reader. The style is complex. However, the style, as very many commentators have pointed out, is loaded with religious symbolism. One can clearly understand the significance of this emotional charge conveyed through the language, but we can also see it from the perspective of those who are not necessarily 'within the Church' and for whom that language remains obscure. As one reads and rereads the text of *Nostra Aetate*, the impression emerges that the Church is speaking to those who are directly a part of it, but that it is ignoring all those 'sons and daughters of the Church' who in theory belong to the Church but in reality are not in it and do not feel part of it. Yet it must be recognised that there is a whole world outside the Church. There is the world of all those who are not theologians, of those who are not pillars of the Church and who nevertheless to some degree identify with a certain number of the Church's traditional teachings. Should they not have found simpler, more inclusive words, more open words, in order to touch the hearts of those who are not within the Church's direct religious sphere and familiar with its complex theology? It would thus appear that there is indeed in this document a certain failure; the failure to address those who are not pillars of the Church or members of the elite but who nevertheless constitute a very substantial percentage of Europe's Christian population. Moreover, we could add that the use of such words, charged as they are with history, spirituality and religious meaning, in a certain way attenuates the revolutionary reach of this text. The spirit of the revolutionary message of the Church's change of direction in its relations with the other religions and with Judaism in particular, seems to me somewhat attenuated and diminished by the use of historically charged words which take us back to former times, times which the Church in the message of this text was at the same time seeking to leave behind.

This type of problem is clearly not specific to the Church and is one we ourselves encounter in Judaism. Let refer to a similar Jewish problematic. Today, when Judaism reflects on certain modern values that are in conflict with traditional teachings, there are two ways of trying to resolve the problem. The first method is to turn to the texts of the *Halakhah*, the Jewish code of law drawn up in the 16th century,[5] and by means of an exercise in intellectual and legal gymnastics, to show that the *Halakhah* has the capacity to adapt to the reality of the modern world. The other approach is to recognise that the *Halakhah* has certain limitations and to acknowledge that it cannot always be adapted to the reality of the modern world. And in order to incorporate the modern world into Judaism, we sometimes have to 'forsake the *Halakhah*' and think outside the traditional tools of our own religion; to think simply with our intelligence, with our commonsense and our goodwill.[6] The choice

---

[5] *Halakhah*, code of Jewish law, based on Biblical quotes and amended and expanded throughout the centuries. The last codification of Jewish Law was compiled in the XVI Century by Rabbi J. Karo in Sefad, Northern Israel. His codification is known as the *shulkah Arukh* and accepted by Jews today.

[6] This attitude has been and still is characteristic of most non orthodox movements in Judaism. Accepting that some changes in the world cannot be reflected

is simple. Either we stay 'inside' and we use the words of tradition, twisted and dragged in every direction in order to make the old texts say what we would like to hear today, or we are prepared to be frankly revolutionary, not only in our thinking but in our methods of thinking, in which case we set aside the old euphemisms and reflect with new words and thoughts. To return to the text of *Nostra Aetate*, there is from a Jewish perspective a feeling that perhaps an aspect of the language of the text that unfortunately seems to run counter to the revolutionary spirit guiding the authors of this text.

The third issue I would like to address, refers more specifically to the theological aspects of the text of *Nostra Aetate*. Jewishly, it is not easy to speak or write about 'theology'. There is not really such a thing as "Jewish theology."[7] Judaism is not a religion of specific dogmas or beliefs but more a religion of practices in which we follow the 613 commandments that God gave to Moses in the text of the Torah.[8] However, while we are not exactly up to speed or great experts in theology, there are nevertheless a certain number of theological points that shock the Jewish reader of the text of *Nostra Aetate*. I would describe the theology of this text as a theology of the 'acceptance of the other' but not a theology of the 'equality of the other'. This text does indeed express an acceptance

by 'traditional words and tools' and must therefore be addressed through a modern approach, inspired by tradition, but clearly separated from its old system of thoughts.

[7] See the introductory words of Arthur Cohen in an essay on "Theology," *Contemporary Jewish Religious Thoughts*, ed. Arthur Cohen and Paul Mendes-Flohr (New York: Free Press, 1998) 971: "Theology in Judaism is an intellectual discipline with a continuous history but a discontinuous tradition. Despite the unbroken productions of works either partly or wholly concerned with the asking of theological questions, the issues they have raised have not always been considered central or even germane to the conduct of Jewish life."

[8] In that respect Judaism is not a 'faith based' religion but rather a 'orthopraxy', a tradition based on the performance of commandments.

of the Jews and of Judaism and of the place of the Jews in the world. But there is not the sense that the Jews are equal, either in law or even in the eyes of God. All that, for a Jewish reader, is clearly shocking and disappointing.

Let me quote a passage of *Nostra Aetate*. "(...) the Church is the new people of God (...)." This short section suggests a concept of election that is very interesting from a Jewish perspective, especially in the 21st century, at a time when the Jewish concept of Israel as the "chosen people"[9] is in radical retreat in Jewish thought.[10] I do not know of any Jewish thinkers today who overtly proclaim the Jews to be 'God's chosen people'. So at a time when the concept of election in the Jewish tradition is losing ground, we find it underlined in the text of *Nostra Aetate*. This is a historical and theological difference that is worth noting.

Let us now turn to a second theological passage in the text of *Nostra Aetate*: "God holds the Jews most dear for the sake of their Fathers (...)." And here one must say quite frankly: 'shocking'. A Jewish reader of this passage has to be 'shocked' by such a statement as we do not understand this theology in which God does not love us as individuals and human beings, but only because of the merit of our ancestors. How is it possible that God does not simply love me as a human being? Could we not have a theology in this text of *Nostra Aetate* in which God loves his children without reference to the past or any particular ancestry? It is shocking to realise that theologically *Nostra Aetate* only accepts the existence of Judaism because of the merits of Abraham. This passage makes us think of a text in the Jewish tradition written by a rabbi called

---

[9] Exodus 19:5 "(...) my treasured possession among all the people" (Li Segulah Mikol Haamim).

[10] See Henri Atlan, "Un people qu'on dit élu," *Le Genre Humain*, nos 2-3 (1982).

Méiri, a great French Rabbi of the Middle Ages, who lived in Provence.[11] He asked himself the same kinds of questions about the Christians. As we all undoubtedly know, in the Jewish tradition Christianity has historically posed a 'theological problem', because the fundamentals of Christianity seemed very close to what rabbis have always considered to be idolatry. For the rabbis, the doctrine of the Trinity was completely incomprehensible and was considered purely and simply as a rejection of monotheism as described in the biblical texts. Similarily the question about Jesus and the 'son of God' theology were harshly criticized by previous rabbinic authorities.[12] Indeed, the Torah is relatively violent towards idolaters and many rabbis over the centuries taught that Christianity was purely and simply idolatry. In the Middle Ages, Méiri taught that although the Trinity is incomprehensible from a Jewish perspective, there was no doubt that the Church is entirely monotheistic and that all Christians are monotheists and should therefore be respected as one of us. Here again, we see the same theory of acceptance and not equality. However, that was a text written in the middle Ages and

[11] Rabbi Menachem ben Solomon Meiri was a provincial scholar and commentator of the Talmud. He summarized the teachings of his predecessors of the previous three centuries. His literary activity covered *halachic* rulings, talmudic exposition, biblical thought, customs, ethics, and philosophy. Meiri summarized the subject matter of the Talmud giving both the meaning and the halakhah derived from it. He utilized all the rabbinic literature available to him, so that his work may be considered a digest which gives a synoptic and comprehensive presentation of the whole expository and halachic activity up to his own time.

[12] See in particular the texts of some "Disputations" in the Middle Ages betweens Jews and Christians. Nahamanides to the Spanish Monarch "that the creator of heaven and earth resorted to the womb of a certain Jewess and grew there for nine months and was born as an infant, and afterward grew up and was betrayed into the hands of his enemies who sentenced him to death and executed him to death and that after ... He came to life and returned to his original place. The mind of a Jew, or any other person, cannot tolerate this." See Rabbi Joseph Telushkin, *Jewish Literacy* (New York: William Morrow, 1991) 188.

not the 20th century. So it could be said that 'Judaism's own *Nostra Aetate*' was written 10 centuries ago, not forty years ago.

Theologically, there is also a profound inequality in the relationship between Judaism and Christianity. The text of *Nostra Aetate* reads: "(…) by His cross Christ (…) reconciled Jews and Christians (…)." Nothing could be further from the truth. Let us simply acknowledge that we Jews do not need Christians in order to live. At a purely religious level, Judaism is self-sufficient. Of course we can take an interest in Christianity, we can take an interest in the affairs of the Church, we can take an interest in the history of the relations between Judaism and Christianity, but our lives as Jews do not depend on what we know about Christianity. So there is an imbalance in the relationship, for on its side the Church needs to return to its Jewish roots to understand itself. That is not the case for our tradition. This same imbalance is clearly present in the responsibility for the other's suffering. The Church, in the aftermath to the Shoah on Christian soil, acknowledges itself to be some degree responsible for the teaching of contempt. Judaism, on the other hand, has nothing to feel guilty about as regards Christianity. The teaching of contempt does not exist in Judaism and never has. In fact, as regards this question, I would like to read you an extract from a book written by the Chief Rabbi of France, Rabbi Jacob Kaplan, reporting a discussion that took place at the Selisberg conference in 1947, which perfectly illustrates this point.[13]

> It was late afternoon. Our committee had met in the open air under the chairmanship of Father Castille Lopinot. On the Christian side, it was agreed that they should acknowledge responsibility for the propagation of anti-Semitism through the teaching of the catechism to young Christians. In return, there was a wish that we too, in a certain way, should recognise a degree of fault on our part towards

---

[13] See Kaplan, *Justice pour la foi juive* (Paris: Le Centurion, 1977) 143.

> Christianity on account of our religious teaching. However, on this
> point, there was nothing to reproach us with. Our books of Jewish
> instruction bear witness. We speak no evil of Christianity, we say
> nothing about it.

As we can see, whether in terms of the theology of acceptance
as against the theology of equality, or the lack of parallelism in
the relationship, the text of *Nostra Aetate* raises a certain number of difficulties for a Jewish reader. This leads us toward the
fourth and final point of this contribution, which I have named:
'the silences'. Indeed what is left unsaid in the text can lead us
to reflect further on the state of relations between the Church and
Judaism.

Two specific points seem to be lacking in the *Nostra Aetate* declaration. The first point concerns the Church itself. Indeed, the word
'Church' is used over and over again in the declaration. But the
children, the sons and daughters of the Church, do not appear there.
So we find here not just an imbalance, but a real 'absence'. An
imbalance, because that the Church is constantly addressing itself
to the 'Jews' and not 'Judaism'. But above all an 'absence', because
one wonders where the "children of the Church" have gone?
Where are those who over the centuries were responsible for the
terrible treatment inflicted upon us? It seems that the *Nostra Aetate*
declaration does not confront the fundamental problem of the
behaviour of the 'children of the Church' and unfortunately remains
rooted in purely theoretical ground, in doctrine. Now it would
appear that today the debate and the combat need to be conducted
at an individual level if we are to have any hope and source of
motivation for the future.

The second factor that seems lacking in the *Nostra Aetate* declaration is obviously Israel, the State of Israel. Nothing about Israel
despite the fact that the declaration dates from 1965 and that at that
time the State of Israel was a well-established reality in the Jewish

world and in the international community. Since then, great advances have been made in this respect and the Vatican has now established diplomatic relations with the State of Israel. Nonetheless, the absence of references to Israel is shocking to a Jewish reader of this text. This lack hurts first of all because the Church needs to accept the reality and the centrality of Israel in Judaism, in the Jewish people and in Jewish thought. And secondly, because the Church must also accept that Judaism only has a future because of Israel and ultimately in Israel. The Jews of the Diaspora in due course have very little future. Many thinkers in our tradition, and some demographers, have concluded that Judaism is inevitably destined to disappear from Europe in the near future.[14] Whether this is as a result of the consequences of the Shoah, of assimilation or simply a lack of interest in our tradition, Diaspora Judaism is on its way out. That is today's harsh reality. So as regards the relations between the Church and Judaism, such relations can only survive through a real recognition of the centrality of Israel, because without Israel, there is no Judaism. Moreover, politics cannot be ignored. We cannot talk about Judaism without reference to today's political problems, which are ultimately at the heart of the relations

---

[14] Let me quote a passage from *The Sacred Chain* by the American Jewish historian Norman Canter. "Demography is destiny," said the eminent British historian Geoffrey Barraclough in the 1960s, and in the case of the Jews, population trends signal the approaching end of Jewish history in Europe as we have known it. 52% of Jewish marriages in the 1990s were intermarriages with Gentiles and since, at best, only one in three non-Jewish spouses convert to Judaism and less that one in three children of these mixed marriages are brought up as Jews, this heralds the steady disappearance of Judaism in Europe. So the picture of European Jewry today is a disheartening one which, to a certain degree, can teach us another lesson: how can such a great culture vanish before our very eyes without us being unable to do anything to prevent it? This is a very depressing issue to contemplate." See Norman Cantor, *The Sacred Chain: A History of the Jews* (New York: Harper Collins Publishers, 1994) 426.

between Jews and the world around us, particularly the Christian world. So it is a pity, disappointing and in fact hard to understand that the State of Israel is totally absent from this declaration.

Let us now finish by attempting to sum up, where we stand today in Jewish-Christian dialogue more than forty years after *Nostra Aetate*. What can we hope for as regards the development of relations between the Church and Judaism?

First of all, it seems that the spirit of courage that inspired the authors of this declaration and the dynamism that they evinced, needs to be reinvented and reinjected into the relations between our two religious traditions. Without courage and without boldness, the relations between religions are difficult and may revert to a condition of dismal stagnation. We need that courage now to confront the real theological difficulties between us. After forty years of dialogue and reciprocal understanding, is it not now time to be ready to tell each other things 'face-to-face', as they really are, and to confront not only the factors that bring us together but also the factors that separate us?

Can the Church accept me as a Jew if I say: "Jesus was a false prophet and means nothing to me?" The statement is shocking and yet it is the core problem in the relations between our two religions. Confronting this type of theological difficulty is a much harder challenge than trying to establish and create links without really daring to raise difficult topics. It means a different degree of tolerance. A degree of tolerance where we are ready to confront problems rather than simply building bridges. In fact, it seems that in the relationship between the Church and Judaism, there is also a need to move from the 'theology of acceptance' to the 'theology of equality'. And for that, both of us, Judaism and the Church need to accept that our religion is not the sole source of Truth. Religiously speaking, can we accept that we do not possess the absolute truth? Are we capable of giving up what we believe to be true in order to acknowledge in the other a morsel of truth equal to our own? Removing the notion of absolute truth from our religions appears to be one of the most important philosophical and religious factors in the development of the dialogue between Judaism and the Church.

We must remember that in the Jewish tradition, the word for truth is: "*Emet.*" Three letters: *aleph, mem, taf.* The first of these three letters, aleph, is unvoiced. If you remove it, two remain: mem and taf, which form the word "*Met,*" death. "Truth" and "death" are two concepts that lie very close together. By continuing to proclaim our absolute truth from the rooftops, do we not risk killing the dialogue between religions?

And should we not also attenuate the notion of election, whether it be the 'chosen people' of the Jewish tradition or the 'new people of God' referred to in the *Nostra Aetate* declaration? By giving up the notion of election, we undoubtedly contribute to building a new theology of equality, which once again seems to me to be the basis for potential development in the relations between our two religions.

Finally, there is the place of Israel in this dialogue. Because without the State of Israel, there's no Judaism. And without Judaism, no Jews. And without Jews, no relationship with the Church.

Let me finish by restating that the Judaeo-Christian dialogue is a necessity in itself. *Nostra Aetate* was only the first step in the re-establishment of relations between our two religions. However, *Nostra Aetate* was never an endpoint. The Judaeo-Christian dialogue is hard and requires courage. But it is a dialogue that carries its own justification, because we live together in Europe and in the world and our two religions have so many things in common, in their past but above all in their future. If I emphasise this point, it is to avoid falling into the trap of believing that this dialogue is simply an adjunct to the Judeo-Muslim dialogue in which the

Church plays the part of moderator, as is often the case today. It seems that it would be dangerous to put the Church in the position of being a 'moderator' rather than at the heart of the dialogue.

I would like to end this contribution with an anecdote about Jules Isaac, who having heard of pope John XXII's plans to reconsider the Church's views on relations with Judaism, asked the pope for an audience in 1960. This audience took place on June 13, 1960. As Jules Isaac left the offices of the Holy See, he asked the pope the following question: "Can I leave this audience with you with a note of hope for my people?" And the Pope replied: "You and we deserve much more than hope."

Today, more than forty years after *Nostra Aetate*, fifty years after the meeting between Jules Isaac and Pope Jean XXIII, the answer and the spirit of the answer have not changed. As regards the relations between the Church and Judaism, all of us deserve more than hope.

THE *NOSTRA AETATE* TRAJECTORY
HOLDING OUR THEOLOGICAL BOW DIFFERENTLY

Mary C. Boys

Nostra Aetate # 4 has been the subject of extensive commentary. This essay constitutes still another contribution to the literature. Two sentences, however, from its second section help to account for my approach:

> The Church, therefore, urges her sons [and daughters] to enter with prudence and charity into discussion [colloquia] and collaboration with members of other religions. Let Christians, while witnessing to their own faith and way of life, acknowledge, preserve and encourage the spiritual and moral truths found among non-Christians, also their social life and culture.

It is unlikely that the Council fathers could have foreseen the breadth and depth of theological exploration that has resulted from serious and sustained engagement with peoples of other religious traditions since 1965. In urging discussion and collaboration, did they grasp the significance of genuine dialogue for Christian self-understanding?

In particular, dialogue with Jews affects how Christians understand their faith because so many Christian teachings have been premised on inadequate notions about Judaism.[1] Once one pulls

---

[1] In the language of *Dialogue and Proclamation* # 42, dialogue takes four forms: the dialogues of life, action, theological exchange, and religious experience. (Text and commentary in *Redemption and Dialogue: Reading Redemptoris Missio and Dialogue and Proclamation,* ed. William R. Burrows (Maryknoll, NY: Orbis, 1993) 104. As I use the term dialogue, in this chapter, I am assuming the expansiveness of all four forms.

out the thread of supersessionism, it becomes necessary to reweave the cloth. Consider, for example, the oft-cited assertion of Pope John Paul II that Jews are a people of the "old covenant, never revoked." So if Jews are still covenanted with God and not, as was taught for centuries, unfaithful and blind, then what, if anything, can or should we say about their salvation? Does their covenanted life with God in any way involve Jesus Christ?

A small international team of Christian scholars gathered in Leuven in August 2007 to think more deeply about our understanding of Christianity in light of our substantial experience of dialogue with Jews.[2] This meeting was called "Christ and the Jewish People" project. The assignment we gave ourselves was to address one question expressed in three variant formulations: "Are Jews saved only by believing in Christ? Are Jews saved without Christ? Are Jews saved without believing in Christ?" This essay is an edited version of my wrestling with the question.

As formulated, the question dared us to probe more analytically and deeply what I assumed our group held in common: God's saving ways extend also to Jews (and beyond the boundaries of Judaism and Christianity, but that is another, if related, topic). It is a challenging question, perhaps in its threefold formulation even a new one on the ancient and complicated topic of soteriology. But was it an appropriate question for us to be addressing? Was it not presumptuous?

When I think of Jews I know who strive to lead lives of integrity in accord with — and inspired by — Torah, I certainly see them as living a life in communion with God (or, perhaps in a more Jewish vocabulary: a life lived in fidelity to Israel's covenant with

---

[2] This was the second meeting of a project we called "Christ and the Jewish People." A larger group of scholars convened in Ariccia, Italy (near Rome) in October 2006. Most of the participants are Roman Catholic; in each meeting Jewish scholars have been present.

God). Empirically, they live the covenant without believing in Jesus. Holiness is obviously possible without belief in Jesus — and so, too, would it seem, is salvation, though what that term means must necessarily become part of our question.

I confess that I think the question demands knowledge we do not have. We neither know the extent of nor the manifold ways in which God "saves," says Michael Barnes, a British Jesuit and scholar of the religions of India. Rather, "the Church speaks of what it knows in faith — that God raised Jesus from the dead and thereby transformed the whole of creation. What the Church does not know is the total reality of what always remains other and utterly mysterious. Christians must, therefore, acknowledge this possibility: God may act in the world in ways of which the Church does not know."[3] As Hanspeter Heinz has said, "all theological questions reaching beyond our historical task may provoke our curiosity, but it is only God's task, not ours, to solve them. Only the eschatological completion of history will [be] the appropriate point of time for an answer."[4]

Whether or not our question was appropriately formulated for the purposes of our "Christ and the Jewish People" project, it is indeed a radical one when situated in the context of Catholic magisterial pronouncements on other religious traditions. Granted, as Cardinal Kasper has argued, Catholic-Jewish relations are not a subset of interreligious relations in general, neither in theory (Judaism is unique among the world's religions because of its theological connection with Christianity) nor in practice (the Commission on Religious Relations with the Jews exists under the

---

[3] Michael Barnes, *Theology and the Dialogue of Religions*, Cambridge Studies in Christian Doctrine (Cambridge: Cambridge University Press, 2002) 28.

[4] Hanspeter Heinz, "What Does it Mean to Claim that Jesus Christ Is the Universal Savior?" (Paper for the Consultation on Christ and the Jewish People, Ariccia, Italy, October 19-22, 2006) 3.

rubric of the Pontifical Council for Christian Unity, not the Pontifical Council for Interreligious Dialogue).[5] Yet recent documents — 'Dialogue and Proclamation' (1991), 'Christianity and World Religions' (1997), and *Dominus Iesus* (2000) — do not treat Judaism in a distinct category. Thus, it is appropriate to situate our question in the larger context, both in looking at our question in light of Catholic doctrinal teachings and of drawing upon some of the work of theologians who write on a theology of religious pluralism.[6]

I begin this essay with a sketch of the 'big picture' of official church teaching, highlighting its development and the unresolved tensions; obviously, one needs a source such as Jacques Dupuis's *Toward a Christian Theology of Religious Pluralism* for a far more detailed and expert analysis.[7] In a word, for centuries the church taught that Jews (and everyone else) could not be saved without belief in Christ and membership in the church. Since Vatican II, the church has affirmed everything that is "true and holy" in other religions (*Nostra Aetate* # 2), and admitted that the salvific action of Christ, with and through the Spirit, extends beyond the visible boundaries of the church to all humanity (*Dominus Iesus* # 12). We might assume the logic of such statements to imply that 'Jews are saved without belief in Christ', though I am dubious that official church teaching would (or should) state this so categorically.

Against the backdrop of this larger framework of church teaching, I will take up possible meanings of 'salvation', and then

---

[5] Cardinal Kasper's address on May 1, 2001 to the International Liaison Committee, as well as the documents issued by the ILC, may be found at www. nccbuscc.org/seia/liaison.htm.

[6] I have limited my focus to the Catholic doctrinal tradition, well aware that Protestant and Orthodox traditions need to be considered as well.

[7] Jacques Dupuis, *Toward a Christian Theology of Religious Pluralism* (Maryknoll, NY: Orbis Books, 1997).

explore some concepts and formulations that might offer us a resource for advancing consideration of the question.

By way of prelude, I suggest an analogy for our theological task. During my early years of teaching at Boston College, a close friend came to live with me while doing an advanced degree in cello performance. She was atypical of her peers in that she was 35 at the time — 'old' to be doing a degree in musical performance. By the time she arrived, she had been playing cello for over a quarter century, including membership for a number of years in her home city's symphony orchestra. Her new mentor, however, taught her to hold the bow differently from how she had held it in the many years of playing cello. I still recall how painful were those first weeks of adjusting to this new position, how a change in something so fundamental reverberated in every aspect of her playing — and eventually, enhanced considerably her performance.

I suggest that *Nostra Aetate* in effect requires the Catholic Church to adjust the bow of its relations with those who are religiously other. This, however, is not a simple alteration. Rather, given how firmly the Church grasped its teaching of contempt and how this grasp so affected fundamentals of our expression of faith, the shift in teaching about Jews and Judaism impinges radically on ecclesial self understanding. It is the call from "exclusion to embrace," to employ Miroslav Volf's metaphor.[8] We must reread and reinterpret and rearticulate our tradition, and this process requires generations of thinking and teaching. The virtues of prudence and charity, recommended in *Nostra Aetate* # 2 are vital for this task, but so, too, is humility.

---

[8] Miroslav Volf, *Exclusion and Embrace: A Theological Exploration of Identity, Otherness, and Reconciliation* (Nashville, TN: Abingdon Press, 1996).

CHRIST, THE CHURCH AND SALVATION

In fact, the documents cited above from the hierarchical magisterium give a firm answer to our question: all persons are saved in Christ. Further, the Church (meaning the Catholic Church) is the ordinary means of salvation, and alone possesses the fullness of salvation. Whatever our perspectives on such a definitive statement, it is crucial to note that the present state of the discussion marks a significant advance over previous declarations.

If it is possible to summarize ecclesiastical teachings briefly without over-simplifying or distorting, it seems to me that the Catholic doctrinal position might be seen as moving in the following manner:[9]

- As central to the kerygma: Jesus Christ is the savior of the world.
- Christ's church is necessary for salvation. That is, 'outside the Catholic Church there is no salvation' (*Extra ecclesiam salus nulla*). This formulation, dating back to Cyprian of Carthage (d. 258) and Fulgentius of Ruspe (468-533), was promulgated for the whole church by the Council of Florence (1438-1442): "The Holy Roman church] firmly believes, professes and preaches that no one remaining outside the Catholic Church, not only pagans," but also "Jews, heretics or schismatics, can become partakers of eternal life; but they will go to the 'eternal fire prepared for the devil and his angels' (Matt 25:41), unless before the end of their life they are received into it ... For union with the body of the Church is of so great importance that the sacraments of the church are helpful to salvation only for those remaining in it; and fasts, almsgiving, other works of piety, and

---

[9] In trying to identify some of the contours of the teaching, I am not suggesting there is trajectory; rather there are movements and counter-movements.

the exercises of a militant Christian life bear eternal rewards for them alone."

- Various theological theories were proffered in order to ameliorate the harshness of the Council of Florence's decree (*e.g.*, baptism of desire, implicit faith, invincible ignorance).

- The Syllabus of Errors (1864) condemned propositions such as: "Everyone is free to embrace and profess the religion which by the light of reason one judges to be true;" and "We should at least have good hopes for the eternal salvation of all those who are in no way in the true Church of Christ."

- When *Nostra Aetate* # 2 spoke of other religious traditions as possessing a "ray of Truth," it was the first time in the history of such doctrinal pronouncements that the Catholic Church spoke positively of other religious traditions.

- Since *Nostra Aetate* (and related statements in *Ad Gentes* and *Gaudium et Spes*), a "bipolarity of tendencies" is evident.[10] On the one hand, there has been striking advancement (*e.g.*, the various documents developing *Nostra Aetate* # 4, the rise of many institutions furthering and deepening interreligious dialogue) and yet on the other, a failure to integrate the insights into central documents such as the *Catechism of the Catholic Church* and *Dominus Iesus*. Indeed, *Dominus Iesus* seemingly requires us to answer that Jews (and everyone else) cannot be saved without Christ, although explicit belief in Christ and membership in the Church are no longer regarded as requisite.[11]

[10] The phrase is from Arthur Gilbert, *The Vatican Council and the Jews* (Cleveland, OH/New York: World Publishing Company, 1968) 215.

[11] "The Church's Magisterium, faithful to divine revelation, reasserts that Jesus Christ is the mediator and the universal redeemer" (# 11). In conclusion, the action of the Spirit is not outside or parallel to the action of Christ. There is only one salvific economy of the One and Triune God, realized in the mystery of the incarnation, death, and resurrection of the Son of God, actualized with the cooperation

- Yet the reception of *Dominus Iesus* has been decidedly mixed, at best.[12] Insofar as reception has become a significant element of magisterial teaching, the status of *DI* is questionable.

The proprietary cast of *Dominus Iesus* calls to mind Daniel Madigan's critique: "It's all ours. We own it. If you want some, you've got to get it from us."[13] The sense that Christianity "owns" salvation, as it were, and that there is no salvation outside the church "makes it seem as though we are talking about having the right answer on the final exam (...) if you can't name the right savior or Messiah when asked, then you're damned."[14] The image of God behind such a proprietary connotation of salvation fails to call persons to the fullness of humanity, and reflects a church lacking in the virtue of humility.

Much of what the church has articulated about Jesus over the centuries has been rooted in a Christology based on supersessionism, and on the refusal to admit the integrity of the Jewish 'no'. Might we at long last acknowledge the consequences of such teaching? As Jewish scholar Peter Ochs says, supersessionism "kills."

---

of the Holy Spirit, and extended in its salvific value to all humanity and to the entire universe: "No one, therefore, can enter into communion with God except through Christ, by the working of the Holy Spirit" (# 12). "It is precisely this uniqueness of Christ which gives him an absolute and universal significance whereby, while belonging to history, he remains history's centre and goal: 'I am the Alpha and the Omega, the first and the last, the beginning and the end' (Rev 22:13)" (# 15).

[12] See Ormond Rush, *Still Interpreting Vatican II: Some Hermeneutical Principles* (Mahwah, NJ: Paulist Press, 2004), who argues that the reception of texts is crucial to their interpretation. See also Stephen J. Pope and Charles C. Hefling (eds.), *Sic et Non: Encountering Dominus Iesus* (Maryknoll, NY: Orbis, 2002).

[13] Daniel Madigan, "How Do We Christians Understand Salvation?" (Paper for the Consultation on Christ and the Jewish People, Ariccia, Italy, October 19-22, 2006) 1.

[14] *Ibid.*, 2.

The "Jewish people in this day must regard a supersessionist church as an obstacle to redemption."[15]

So we struggle now with a language based on premises we can in justice and truth no longer accept. Moreover, many formulas about Jesus as the one savior of all humankind are of the genre of confessional language that takes on a different character when pressed too analytically.

Barnes speaks of the vulnerability that partners in interreligious dialogue experience; we are always faced with "irreducible otherness." Accordingly, he calls for a theology that allows for "passivity," that is, a sort of contemplative apophasis arising out of the experience of "limitation imposed by otherness of all kinds."[16] Might not our inability to reconcile fully ancient claims of Christian faith with our post-*Nostra Aetate* understandings of Judaism lead us to greater humility about our tradition and draw us more deeply into the *mysterium salutis?* Might not our vulnerability in the face of Jewish otherness be an inability to speak with assurance with a 'panoptic' vision of God's actions in the world?

Perhaps it is the "irreducible otherness" that the hierarchical magisterium cannot accept. Instead, it speaks with a definitive voice, as if nothing had been learned from ecumenical and interreligious dialogue, as if it were absolutely sure of its panoptic vision. Nor has it listened to Didier Pollefeyt's plaintive argument:

---

[15] Peter Ochs, "Israel's Redeemer," *The Redemption*, ed. Stephen T. Davis, Daniel Kendall, SJ and Gerald O'Collins, SJ (Oxford: Oxford University Press, 2004) 145.

[16] Barnes, *Theology and the Dialogue of Religions*, 23. "The question for a theology of dialogue is not how the otherness revealed at the heart of selfhood can be synchronized into a more or less grand strategy, but how, more radically and yet more humbly, a certain passivity in the face of the other is to be recognized as *intrinsic* to the Christian vocation itself" (129).

"Auschwitz means the definitive end of Christological salvation triumphalism."[17]

SALVATION: ENLARGING OUR IMAGINATION

From the outset we need to admit that 'salvation' is a much more complicated and textured term than is apparent from theological shorthand. 'Jesus saves' is a significant claim of our faith, but its brevity belies layers of metaphors, biblical and liturgical formulae, and doctrinal arguments.

Although the Church has pronounced with confidence that Jesus is the "Word of God made man for the salvation of all," and sees itself as having been entrusted by God with "the fullness of grace and truth," it has never formally defined the meaning of salvation. In his *Toward a Christian Theology of Religious Pluralism*, Dupuis explores in detail Catholic thought about the salvation of those beyond its borders while saying little about what the church understood salvation to be. Nor does Dupuis himself offer much speculation about the nature of salvation.[18] As Roger Haight remarks, the meaning of salvation is elusive: "Every intentional Christian knows what salvation is until asked to explain it."[19] Two theologians do try to offer some illumination by formulating brief definitions of salvation. Philip Cunnigham defines salvation as "being in a relationship with God that involves the ongoing acceptance, as individuals and communities, of God's invitation to participate in

[17] Didier Pollefeyt, "Christology After Auschwitz: A Catholic Perspective," (http://jcrelations.net/en/index.php?id=775&format).

[18] Dupuis speaks of salvation/liberation as "it has to do with the search for, and attainment of, fullness of life, wholeness, self-realization, and integration" Dupuis, *Toward a Christian Theology*, 306-307.

[19] Roger Haight, *Jesus: Symbol of God* (Maryknoll, NY: Orbis1999) 335.

God's unfolding plans for the world (plans that will eventually lead to the Reign of God, the Age to Come. Relationships that generate this participation are 'salvific.' People are 'saved' from sin, meaninglessness, and death by this sharing-in-life with God and are set on a path of reconciliation, holiness, and steadfast love."[20] Daniel Madigan offers the following definition of salvation: "In the Christian understanding, being saved means being incorporated into the divine life through the person of the fully divine, fully human one. This incorporation takes place by the gracious initiative of God, who invites a free human response. Wherever we can discern this response taking place, we are witnessing salvation — including outside the visible confines of the Church."[21]

Both of these definitions offer a wider horizon for reflection than does the nearly exclusive focus on the death of Jesus as 'the' saving event. Excessive emphasis on the crucifixion as the salvific act removes it from its historical matrix in Roman-ruled Palestine, and obscures the salvific dimension of Jesus' teachings and resurrection:

> Herein lies the saving power of this event: death does not have the last word. The crucified one is not annihilated but brought to new life in the embrace of God, who remains faithful in surprising ways. Thereby the judgment of earthly judges is reversed and Jesus' own person, intrinsically linked with his preaching and praxis, is vindicated.[22]

[20] Philip Cunningham, "How Do We Christians Think of Salvation?" (Paper for the Consultation on Christ and the Jewish People, Ariccia, Italy, October 19-22, 2006) 2.

[21] Madigan, "How Do We Christians Understand Salvation?," 2.

[22] Elizabeth Johnson, "The Word Was Made Flesh and Dwelt Among Us: Jesus Research and Christian Faith," *Jesus: A Colloquium in the Holy Land*, ed. Doris Donnelly (New York/London: Continuum, 2001) 157. Much more needs to be said about both the rich resonances of terms in the First Testament and the historical context of the death of Jesus — but not in this essay.

Situating salvation in a broader horizon of thought suggests at least three implications. First, it emphasizes Jesus as a prophet who, despite opposition and danger, continued to preach and emulate God's reign. While we will never fully know what Jesus experienced in Gethsemane, it seems probable that he spent the night in an agonized discernment about what he was called to — to go underground in order to continue his ministry, or to accept the consequences of his witness to a God whose gracious and generous love was extended to all, even (or especially) to those whom the Roman Empire regarded as of no consequence. It is not that God needed the crucifixion of Jesus as a sacrificial atonement, but rather that God desired that what Jesus said and did would flourish: "Human sin thwarted this divine desire yet did not defeat it."[23] Moreover, as Josef Wohlmuth has stated, the "God of Israel prior to all ecclesiastical activities has decided the salvation of Israel."[24]

To contemplate Jesus' prophetic witness enables us to make connections to our broken world in which people at the margins of society still suffer. We know people in our own day who, despite opposition and danger, nevertheless carry on their advocacy for a more just society, even if they suffer death because of it. Their memory inspires and sustains us because, like Jesus, they were willing to carry on for a cause greater than themselves, a cause furthering God's reign on earth. In their passionate commitment to counter evil in its varied and powerful manifestations, they mediate the divine care for creation. These 'saints' exemplify God's desire for the flourishing of all, human and non-human. They are participants in the divine drama of salvation.

---

[23] Johnson, "The Word Was Made Flesh and Dwelt Among Us," 158.

[24] Josef Wohlmuth, "What Is the Relationship between the Death of Jesus and Salvation" (Paper for the Consultation on Christ and the Jewish People, Ariccia, Italy, October 19-22, 2006) 4.

Second, thinking in such a fashion places the emphasis on God's solidarity with human suffering rather than on Jesus' death as a self-offering to God. This latter notion of 'penal substitution' in which Jesus bore the punishment God would otherwise have inflicted on us, and by so doing turned God's hostility away from us, reflects an abhorrent image of the Divine. As Douglas John Hall writes in regard to the second side of the 'revelations of Calvary':

> That Jesus Christ was crucified was no more the direct will and plan of God than that a million innocent children should have been slain in the Holocaust. To put forward the events of Holy Week as a kind of divinely predetermined Oberammergau play whose author and director is none other than Almighty God is to have substituted for biblical faith a fatalism that may belong to Stoicism, but not to the tradition of Jerusalem. Afterwards — but only then — faith is allowed to see the hand of God in this human tragedy.(…) And no kind of theology, no high-minded desire to uphold the sovereignty of God, can be allowed here if it has the effect of distracting human attention away from the reality of our own distortedness by making God the puppeteer who pulled the strings of Christ's executioners.[25]

Third, situating salvation in the full sweep of the life, death and resurrection enables us to enter into the varied metaphors of the New Testament. In Christ we are healed, we are set free, we are ransomed, we are reborn as God's children, we are reconciled to God and one another, and we are justified. 'Salvation' is an encompassing term, one best entered into by poetic cast of mind in which metaphors retain their sense of strangeness and mystery.

Contemporary biblical scholarship on Jesus, Elizabeth Johnson argues, has the capacity to affect faith insofar as it changes the

---

[25] See Douglas John Hall, *The Cross in Our Context: Jesus and the Suffering World* (Minneapolis, MN: Fortress, 2003) 103-104.

Christian imagination by offering new 'memory images'. In offering new ways of seeing Jesus, biblical scholars invite the church to
enter imaginatively into:

> Jesus the Jew; a marginal Jew; a prophet of Israel's restoration; a
> Spirit-filled leader, compassionate healer, subversive sage, and a
> founder of a revitalization movement within Judaism; a Mediter-
> ranean Jewish peasant; an eschatological prophet proclaiming the
> dawning of the reign of God and paying the price with his life —
> these various profiles are changing the traditional Christian imagi-
> nation regarding the dynamic of Jesus' life and destiny.[26]

Jesper Svartvik suggests that presenting Jesus' proclamation of the
coming reign of God and his passion as complementary offer us a
portrait of the "totality of Jesus of Nazareth as the expression and
revelation of God." Svartvik criticizes excessive focus on the reconciliation on the cross as leading to the assertion that Jesus' principal reason for his existence was to die for us. Likewise, he takes
issue with placing too much emphasis on revelation, thereby
removing Jesus from his Jewish matrix. Like John Pawlikowski, he
believes an incarnational theology best does justice to Jesus as a
reflection of the divine.[27] Pawlikowski defines incarnational theology as resting on the argument that "Christ's salvific work begun

[26] Johnson, "The Word Was Made Flesh and Dwelt Among Us," 150. Johnson uses the term "Jesus research" to summarize a "fresh renaissance in Jewish
studies" in which historical and literary criticism are complemented by methods
from the social studies. She realizes, of course, that some of these images drawn
from scholars in "Jesus research" stand in tension with one another; still, she
claims, they "encapsulate an awareness of the figure at the origin of Christianity
different from that of the doctrinal Christ of traditional piety" (151).

[27] Jesper Svartvik, "Forging an Incarnational Theology," *Studies in Jewish-
Christian Relations* 1 (2005-2006) 1-13, esp. 13. Brian Daley suggests something similar in his claim that "God must work out salvation by becoming one
of us, rather than by acting through a creature (such as the Arian Christ) delegated
to do his work in the world, simply because salvation cannot be conceived simply as 'work', however dramatic and however providential. The reason, as the

in the historical mission of Jesus is accomplished primarily through ... the enhanced transparency of the divine link with humanity made present through God's integration into humanity in and through Jesus and the implications of this for the deepening, continuing divine reign in human history."[28]

In many popular understandings of salvation in our culture, however, so much prominence is given to the death of Jesus that both incarnation and resurrection are largely overlooked. But the resurrection is integrally connected to the ministry, passion, and death; the cross as we know it is that of the Risen One who is Emmanuel.

Roger Haight suggests that the salvific power of the resurrection is best understood by correlating it with the human experience of transcendental hope, "a radical openness of the human spirit to being into the future." Jesus' death "as a death into resurrection amounts to a promise by God of salvation in the future that responds to human hope (...) The future now becomes a real dimension of being for the person who transcends living 'only in order to die.'"[29]

Even when salvation is used in the present tense — "Jesus saves" — it seems to be a reality already accomplished. Emphasizing the "already" over the "not yet" obscures the eschatological horizon and permits us to be passive recipients of salvation.

Fathers intuitively grasped, is that salvation simply is God's personal presence among us as 'Emmanuel'. Only by that presence does he begin in our human nature and community the process of purification and transformation that in the end allows us to be fully present to God: as sons and daughters with the Son, in the power of the Holy Spirit as participants in God's life and inner relationships, 'sharers in the divine nature'." ("He Himself Is Our Peace," *The Redemption*, 175-176.

[28] John Pawlikowski, "What Does it Mean to Claim That Jesus Christ Is Constitutive to Salvation?" (Paper for the Consultation on Christ and the Jewish People, Ariccia, Italy, October 19-22, 2006) 2.

[29] Haight, *Jesus*, 347-348.

"Salvation," Barbara Brown Taylor writes, "is not about earthlings going up but about heaven coming down, and any notion of salvation that does not include just rulers, honest judges, an equitable economy, and peace among nations, would have made Isaiah scratch his head."[30] Or as she says in a more recent work:

> Based entirely on my reading of scripture, it seems entirely possible that Jesus might define salvation as recovery from illness or addiction, as forgiveness of debt, as peace between enemies, as shared food in time of famine, or as justice for the poor. These are all outbreaks of health in a sin-sick world. Jesus saves because he shows us how to multiply such outbreaks, and because he continues to be present in them.[31]

Perhaps the Reformation debates about faith and works have contributed to a certain disconnect between salvation in Christ and Christian practices. Whatever the cause, it seems vital in our time that we communicate more vividly ways in which walking the 'Way of Jesus' saves us. Claims that Christians alone will be saved obscure the powerful message of the gospel: God-with-us has given us in Christ a way of living that saves us from excessive self-absorption, fear and enslavement. In living as disciples, we not only experience salvation but also act in ways that contribute to the world's salvation. Discipleship calls us to turn away from the destructiveness of sin.

To say that God saves us through Jesus Christ is in large measure to claim that Jesus invites us to a Way to God that patterns our daily lives. Graced by his Spirit, we are enabled to experience salvation. By striving to love our enemies, we lessen the world's violence and the violence within our own being. By engaging in acts

[30] Barbara Brown Taylor, "Easter Preaching and the Lost Language of Salvation," *Journal for Preachers* (Easter 2002) 20.

[31] Id., *Speaking of Sin: The Lost Language of Salvation* (Cambridge, MA: Cowley Publications, 2000).

of foot-washing and table service, we are redeemed from the con-striction of selfishness and become part of activity larger than our-selves — an activity that partakes of the coming reign of God. By forgiving others (and ourselves), we experience deliverance from an anger that can so easily corrode us by sapping our psychic energy. By responding to those in need, we mediate God's healing.

We need to extend the horizon of our imagination in thinking about salvation, to see it, in the words of Brazilian theologian Ivone Gebara, as a "dynamic movement in the innermost part of our lives," as our hope for creation itself, as communion of persons with God. While we may speak of various difficulties in our lives as a "cross," we tend to be more reticent about noting times of resurrection. Gebara writes that the "process of salvation is a process of resur-rection, of recovering life and hope and justice along life's path even though these experiences are frail and fleeting. Resurrection becomes something that can be lived and grasped within the confines of our existence." She observes that "there is a whole spirituality focused on the elemental things of life, in friendships, in the little joys of every day that lead to feelings of gratitude and gratuitousness."[32]

Gebara, who lives and work with some of Brazil's poorest, speaks of the necessity of searching for salvation each day, of view-ing salvation as redemption in the here and now of our bodies and daily routines. Salvation, she says, is everywhere — even in the hell of suffering — and present everywhere "under different forms, inviting us to go beyond the evil or despondency that torments us." Gebara rightly says that claiming the "dailiness" of salvation does not deny the perspective of "the beyond of history." There is always a tension, so we must take care not to "affirm the beyond at the expense of actual history."

---

[32] Ivone Gebara, *Out of the Depths: Women's Experience of Evil and Salva-tion*, trans. Ann Patrick Ware (Minneapolis, MN: Fortress, 2002) 122-124.

Were we to lay claim to the 'everyday' character of salvation, we might begin to connect salvation to taking up our cross — that is, that God asks us to participate in the world's salvation by giving freely of our lives to others, to engage in 'salvific activity' in innumerable ways. "There is no salvation apart from being in relation with other human beings."[33]

Would not such understandings of salvation help Christians connect their belief in Christ with the world in which they live rather than think of salvation as what Christ achieved for us on the cross: heaven?

Conversing with Theologians of Religious Pluralism

In a sense, three "schools" of theological literature are at play in this chapter. The first, largely assumed but deeply embedded in my thinking, is what we might call the post-*Nostra Aetate* trajectory, consisting not simply of the trail of official Church teachings on Jews and Judaism since 1965 but also of the large body of commentary, analysis and (re)interpretation.

The second, generally in tension with this trajectory, consists of statements from the hierarchical magisterium such as *Dominus Iesus* and its recent clarification in June 2007.[34] Fidelity to the post-*Nostra Aetate* trajectory makes it difficult, if nearly impossible, to assent to the assumptions, methods, and conclusions of the second 'school'. Given recent decisions from the Congregation for the Doctrine of the Faith, such as the notification to Jesuit Jon Sobrino,

[33] Haight, *Jesus*, 356.

[34] The clarification is from the Congregation of the Faith, "Responses to Some Questions Regarding Certain Aspects of the Doctrine on the Church," promulgated June 29, 2007.

this difference in assumption and methodology between the *Nostra Aetate* and certain Vatican authorities is a cause for concern.[35]

The third, the subject of a very brief review in this section, centers around recent Christian theological explorations on religious pluralism. The literature here is burgeoning, much of it from Asia, where Christians constitute only 3 percent of the population, and from scholars deeply immersed in other cultures and religious traditions. This literature is also characterized by substantial differences in method and arguments, so it is important not to generalize about "pluralistic theology."[36]

Let me begin with an observation. Scholars and pastors from the first and third groups, although typically not conversant with the other's literature, share one especially vital connection: profound relationships with the religious 'other.' We know something not

[35] See Scott Appleby, "American Idol: The 'Modernist' Crisis Revisited," *Commonweal* 134/15 (September 14, 2007) 12-20, 20. Appleby, while acknowledging that the papacies of John Paul II and Benedict XVI differ significantly from the anti-Modernist papacies of Pius IX and Pius X, sees the ad hominem attacks on "dissenting Catholic intellectuals" by the Popes Pius echoed in the actions of the present pope and his predecessor. Appleby asks, "Have we moved beyond the Modernist/anti-Modernist polarities of a century ago, in which the range of acceptable theological resources is restricted to one historically significant but by no means exclusively orthodox school of thought?" He concludes: "After change upon changes, one fears, we are more or less the same."

[36] Here I take issue with Pollefeyt's assertion that "Pluralism reduces religions to relative and exchangeable human constructions or interpretations and denies the particularities of religions and the attachments and loyalties of it members to it." Didier Pollefeyt, "What Does it Mean to Claim that Jesus Christ Is Constitutive of Salvation?" (Paper for the Consultation on Christ and the Jewish People, Ariccia, Italy, October 19-22, 2006) 5. I agree that this is the case with some approaches to religious pluralism (*e.g.*, that of John Hick, the threefold typology of exclusivism, inclusivism, and pluralism), but it is not accurate of others (*e.g.*, those who work as comparativists, whose goal is to deepen an understanding of Christianity through engagement with the persons and thinking of other religious traditions).

only about Judaism or Buddhism or Hinduism, but also about real Jews, Buddhists and Hindus. We write not only from the library, but also from the other side of the Shabbat table or out of the practice of Zen or from reading the Upanishads alongside Hindus or from work together for peace and justice.[37] As friends and colleagues, we are privileged to receive glimpses of the power of another religious tradition at work in the lives of real people.[38] Moreover, our relationships have given us a keen sense of how harmful Christian superiority — often combined with a colonial arrogance — has been to real peoples.[39] In contrast, a statement such as *Dominus Iesus* is written from metaphysical perch; it assumes a position of omniscience for which the experience of dialogue and interreligious friendships are irrelevant.[40]

[37] Dupuis claims that the point of departure for a theology of religious pluralism is the praxis of interreligious dialogue: "Such a theology, in effect, does not look at the praxis of interreligious dialogue merely as a necessary condition, premise, or even a first step; it further maintains a dialogical attitude at every stage of the reflection; it is theological reflection *on* and *within* dialogue" (*Toward a Christian Theology of Religious Pluralism*, 19). Ironically, however, he makes virtually no reference to his own nearly forty years in India in this lengthy book, which was censured by the Congregation for the Doctrine of the Faith.

[38] See James Fredericks, "Interreligious Friendship: A New Theological Virtue," *Journal of Ecumenical Studies* 35/2 (1998) 168-172.

[39] Rasiah Sugirtharajah writes: "Along with gunboats, opium, slaves and treaties, the Christian Bible became a defining symbol of European expansion" (*The Bible and the Third World* [Cambridge: Cambridge University Press, 2001] 13).

[40] As an example of the dangers of *Dominus Iesus*: "Imagine, for instance, that you are in Nigeria, a country with a longstanding and violent history of conflict between its Muslim north and Christian south. Suppose you inform a Muslim Nigerian, with full fervor and conviction, that in comparison with Catholics he is in 'a gravely deficient situation' with regard to salvation. What is the chance of your convincing him of the salvific advantages of the Catholic Church — a church whose primary meaning to him may be that it once led the Crusades and is currently awash in sexual scandal? How would you answer if he countered your assertion with the Saudi textbook's assertion that 'every religion other than Islam

Particularly on the topic of soteriology and its relation to Jews, we might benefit from listening in on theologies of religious pluralism without losing the distinctiveness of Christianity's relationship with Judaism.[41] Here I offer just a few possibilities.

As we address the question of the 'Christ and the Jewish People' project, we might pause before Mark Heim's argument that religions have different ends. Salvation, therefore, properly must be spoken of in the plural, as does his book title.[42] It may be that Nirvana and communion with God are different ends for Buddhists and Christians, but, we might object, is not salvation indeed the same end for both Jews and Christians, particularly since the term itself arises out of biblical Israel? Heim would, I think, disagree, since he defines salvation in the Christian tradition in a subsequent work as "true communion with the triune God," and regards it as the greatest of all ends.[43] Yet Heim sees the Trinity as a warrant for pluralism, since it images the pluralism within the Divine.

Whatever one thinks of Heim's arguments, his work challenges us to probe various Jewish and Christian understandings of salvation, and of its related terms, such as redemption, reconciliation,

---

is false'? Such an exchange might exacerbate the already violent tension between Nigerian Muslims and Christians. Unless it is deeply rooted in genuine and sincere dialogues of life, action, and religious experience, your description of his religious condition, inspired by an innocent affirmation of an ecclesiastical document such as *Dominus Iesus*, would be the equivalent of shouting "Fire" in a crowded theater." Peter Phan, "Praying to the Buddha: Living Amid Religious Pluralism," *Commonweal* 134/2 (January 26, 2007) 12.

[41] The most incisive typology and analysis of the varying perspectives is Paul F. Knitter, *Introducing Theologies of Religion* (Maryknoll, NY: Orbis Books, 2002).

[42] Mark Heim, *Salvations: Truth and Difference in Religions* (Maryknoll, NY: Orbis Books, 1995).

[43] Id., *The Depth of the Riches: A Trinitarian Theology of Religious Ends* (Grand Rapids, MI: Eerdmans, 2001). This work, as the one previously cited, is richly nuanced and deserving of greater explication than I can do here.

and atonement. As we do so, we need to be cognizant that Jews and Christians are separated by a common nomenclature. Svartvik says: "To complicate things even more, it is argued here that Jews and Christians have more in common when they do not use a common terminology, *i.e.*, *mitzwot*, *sacramentum*, *Torah*, incarnation. I also propose that they misunderstand each other because, at times, they share a common terminology, *i.e.*, 'Law', 'Messianism', 'good deeds'. All this suggests that it is important to identify the fundamental points of agreement. Jews and Christians need to be reminded of what they have in common — even if separated by a common nomenclature."[44]

It may well be that the term 'salvation', which we inherited from biblical Israel, is a case study in 'separation by a common nomenclature'. Nevertheless, Rabbi Sybil Sheridan argues:

> I hope to have demonstrated that despite the many perceptions to the contrary, Judaism's theology parallels many of the notions of salvation held by the Catholic Church. Regarding the question of national or personal salvation, it becomes evident that despite the language, and the experience in history, the Jewish understandings of salvation are nevertheless personal and relate to the individual and their God. On the question of the need for salvation it becomes clear that Judaism contains within it its own notion of original sin, located in the internal *yetser hara* or in the external *kelippot* the flaws of the universe. I am confident, that Catholic theologians today embarking on the same exercise could find essentially Judaic elements in their theologies of salvation.[45]

Sheridan does not dissolve differences. Jewish perspectives on salvation, which vary significantly, tend to place more emphasis on

---

[44] Jesper Svartvik, "'It is Not Too Late To Seek a Newer World' — Why Jewish-Christian Relations Matter," Public Lecture held on March 7, 2007, at Paideia, The European Institute for Jewish Studies in Sweden.

[45] Rabbi S. Sheridan, "Salvation: The Four Questions" (Paper for the Theology of Partnership Conference, London, May 18-20, 2003) 17.

the existential or unredeemed dimension. And no matter how much Jews might come to reconsider Jesus in the matrix of Second Temple Judaism, they will never regard him as "Savior."

We might also look to some of the formulations of our colleagues in theologies of pluralism as we take up this question of Jews and salvation? At best we might find, in David Tracy's memorable phrase, "relatively adequate" language — but might we not benefit from taking a hard look at, for example, this formulation of Paul Knitter:

> Jesus bears a 'universal, decisive and indispensable' message, even though he is not God's full, definitive and unsurpassable truth. Jesus is universal insofar as his life bears witness to a revelation of God's saving truth that bears significance to human beings of every culture and religious commitment. He is decisive insofar as the truth revealed in his proclamation of God's reign summons us to make an irrevocable decision about ourselves and the way we will spend our lives in this world. He is indispensable insofar as the truth of other religious traditions can be enhanced and clarified through encountering the good news revealed in Jesus.[46]

Might we find in the Knitter formulation a resonance of Schubert Ogden's distinction between a constitutive and a representative understanding of salvation in Jesus? In the former, the life and work of Jesus constitute salvation, bringing it in a way that no other can. In the latter, Jesus represents the possibility of salvation, which God's primordial and everlasting love brings about.[47]

Finally, might we look to the Asian bishops? Admittedly, theirs is a radically different context. Yet their reluctance to continue

---

[46] Paul Knitter, "Five Theses Regarding the Uniqueness of Jesus," *The Uniqueness of Jesus: A Dialogue with Paul Knitter*, ed. Leonard Swidler and Paul Mojzes (Maryknoll, NY: Orbis, 1997) 3-16.

[47] See Pollefeyt, "What Does it Mean to Claim that Jesus Christ Is Constitutive of Salvation?," 5-6.

speaking of Jesus as the sole Savior of the world in favor of relating to and including other truths seems relevant to our own commitments. Asian Catholics, according to Cardinal Julius Darmaatmadja of Indonesia, favor speaking about Jesus as the "Teacher of Wisdom, the Healer, the Liberator, the Compassionate Friend of the Poor, the Good Samaritan" rather than as the "one and only Son of God and Savior."[48]

I acknowledge the ecclesiastical risks of entering into conversation with such theologians of religious pluralism. In our time, however, bold perseverance in the dialogue is called for. And has not our own engagement with Jews and Judaism deepened and enlivened our own practice of Christianity — and thereby proved salutary?

So we cannot turn aside from all that we have learned from dialogue — in the full breadth and depth of that experience — with Jews. Not only prudence and charity, but also humility, demand ecclesiastical reticence in specifying how Jews are saved. The experience of dialogue demands that we articulate our understanding of Christ as profoundly and faithfully as we can, but surely fidelity to the *Nostra Aetate* trajectory also entails confession of and repentance for the ways in which our claim 'Jesus saves' has had tragic consequences for Jews.

Over twenty-five years ago, the bishops of France spoke of the Jewish people as posing questions to Christians that "touch on the heart of our faith."[49] Yes, dialogue with Jews indeed brings more questions, even unsettling ones. And did not a Jew from Nazareth ask, "Who do you say that I am?" Our pursuit of more adequate

---

[48] Cited in Knitter, *Introducing Theologies of Religion*, 98.

[49] Statement by the French Bishops' Committee for Relations with Jews, April 1973, *Stepping Stones to Further Jewish-Christian Relations*, ed. Helga Croner (New York/London: Stimulus Books, 1977) 60.

ways of addressing questions that arise from the experience of dialogue enlivens our theology and challenges us to live our beliefs.

ISRAEL AND THE CHURCH
FULFILLMENT BEYOND SUPERSESSIONISM?

Marianne MOYAERT & Didier POLLEFEYT

INTRODUCTION

In the history of the Jewish-Christian relationships, Christians have often wondered whether or not the Church has replaced Israel as God's chosen people. Can Israel, after the coming of Christ, the Son of God, still be considered 'the people of God'? A negative answer to this question is usually described as 'substitution theology', 'replacement theology', or as 'supersessionist theology' (from the Latin *supersedere:* 'to be superior to'). Christians assumed that, by their belief in Jesus as Messiah, the election of the Jewish people had been definitively and exclusively transferred to them.[1] For once and for all, the Church had taken the place that used to belong to Judaism. The implication of this theology is that there is no longer a place for Israel in God's salvific plan. Israel's role in the history of revelation and salvation has ended forever. The Jewish 'no' to Jesus as Messiah meant the end of God's commitment to Israel. The new chosen people, the true, spiritual Israel, and the new covenant now take central place. In keeping with this theology, Christian exegesis, liturgy, and catechesis have represented the

---

[1] Didier Pollefeyt, "In Search of an Alternative for the Theology of Substitution," *Jews and Christians: Rivals or Partners for the Kingdom of God? In Search of An Alternative for the Christian Theology of Substitution*, ed. Didier Pollefeyt, (Leuven: Peeters, 1998) 1-9.

relation between the first and second testament in terms of old and new, temporary and definitive, shadow and reality. The idea behind these supersessionist expressions is that Israel lost its privileged status as God's chosen people at the moment she rejected God's invitation in Christ. Because of this, Israel lost its right of existence; it is now a cursed nation or, at best, anachronistic.

Substitution theology is based on the premise of a christomonist understanding of salvation. Exclusivist theology is based on the belief that there is only one covenant, one gospel, and one redeemer, namely Jesus Christ. Access to salvation is exclusively linked to the conviction that Christ is the Savior on God's behalf. The thesis that the Jews had already made a covenant with God, one that would make Christ superfluous for their salvation, is rejected. Even stronger, Jews who do not recognize Christ as Messiah are lost. Exclusivism is not only christomonist but also ecclesiomonist by nature. Indeed, belonging to the one, true, Catholic Church is understood as the criterion needed to achieve the state of grace. 'No salvation outside the Church'. The Church that christ founded, substituted Israel as God's salvific instrument. Hence the Church needs to proclaim the gospel to the Jews as well.

Substitution theology played a prominent role in Christian thinking from an early period. It is no surprise therefore that for centuries this theology formed an undisputed element of Christian teaching both in the Western and in the Eastern churches. To the Church, it was a source of annoyance that the Jews rejected Jesus as Messiah and that they did not recognize that their role in God's salvific plan had been definitively played out. For almost two thousand years the Church has given expression to this annoyance through anti-Jewish statements and deeds. Even if Nazism should not be understood as an inevitable and direct outcome of Christendom — as accepted by the Jewish document *Dabru Emet*

(2000)[2] it is nevertheless obvious that without the long history of Christian anti-Jewish perspective and the anti-Jewish acts of violence that followed, the Nazi ideology would never have been able to take root and it would certainly not have been imitated so fanatically in the heart of European civilization.[3]

Certainly, it is no exaggeration to assert that the *Shoah*, insofar it forms the climax of a longstanding tradition of anti-Jewish discrimination against the Jewish people, contains one the most important inducements for the "revolutionary change"[4] in the Church's attitude vis-à-vis Israel.[5] Particularly the Second Vatican Council (1962-1965) brought about a turning point in

[2] *Dabru Emet* can be found (with commentaries by Jewish and Christians scholars) in Tikva Frymer-Kensky, David Novak, Peter Ochs, David Fox Sandmel, and Michael Signer (eds.), *Christianity in Jewish Terms* (Boulder, CO: Westview Press, 2000).

[3] Zie ook Joseph Ratzinger, "The Heritage of Abraham: The Gift of Christmas," *L'Osservatore Romano,* 29 December, 2000. "We know that every act of giving birth is difficult. Certainly, from the very beginning, relations between the infant Church and Israel were often marked by conflict. The Church was considered by her own mother to be a degenerate daughter, while Christians considered their mother to be blind and obstinate. Down through the history of Christianity, already-strained relations deteriorated further, even giving birth in many cases to anti-Jewish attitudes, which throughout history have led to deplorable acts of violence. Even if the most recent, loathsome experience of the *Shoah* was perpetrated in the name of an anti-Christian ideology, which tried to strike the Christian faith at its Abrahamic roots in the people of Israel, it cannot be denied that a certain insufficient resistance to this atrocity on the part of Christians can be explained by an inherited anti-Judaism present in the hearts of not a few Christians."

[4] David M. Gordis, "John Paul II on the Jews," *John Paul II and Interreligious Dialogue*, ed. Byron L. Sherwin & Harold Kasimow (Maryknoll, NY: Orbis, 1999) 125-138, 125.

[5] Massimo Guiliani, "The Shoah as a Shadow upon and a Stimulus to Jewish-Christian Dialogue," *The Catholic Church and the Jewish People: Recent Reflections from Rome*, ed. P. A. Cunningham, N. J. Hofmann & J. Sievers (New York: Fordham University Press, 2007) 54-72.

Jewish-Christian relationships. As far as the Church's attitude towards Judaism is concerned, the Council's intentions lay mainly in the stimulation of new relations of mutual understanding and respect as well as dialogue and cooperation. One of the Council's purposes was to gather an as large as possible majority in favor of a changing attitude of the Church vis-à-vis the Jews.[6] It was presupposed that an open attitude towards Judaism would become possible only on the basis of a positive theological appreciation of Israel.

Particularly, the conciliar document *Nostra Aetate* has played an unmistakably important role in the changing relationship between the Church and the Jewish people.[7] *Nostra Aetate* recognizes that the relations between the Church and Israel were characterized by ignorance, conflict, and confrontation for almost two thousand years. The document expresses the hope that, in the future, the bonds between Jews and Christians can evolve beyond apologetics towards dialogue and encounter. To that end, *Nostra Aetate* confirms the strong liaison among the Church and the Jewish people and it calls Christians to reject the old anti-Judaism and anti-Semitism.

With the declaration of the conciliar document *Nostra Aetate*, the Church tries to break away from the exclusivist substitution theology and the "teaching of contempt."[8] The text clearly recognizes the intrinsic and lasting significance of Judaism. "Jews remain faithful to God," even though this recognition is immediately modified: "because of the patriarchs." "The Church," according to *Nostra Aetate*, "cannot forget that she received the

---

[6] Jacques Dupuis, *La rencontre du christianisme et des religions: De l'affrontement au dialogue* (Paris: Cerf, 2002) 99.

[7] Pollefeyt, "Jews and Christians after Auschwitz: From Substitution to Inter-religious Dialogue," 21.

[8] Jules Isaac, *The Teaching of Contempt: Christian Roots of Anti-Semitism* (New York: Holt, 1964).

revelation of the Old Testament through the people with whom God, in His inexpressible mercy, concluded the Ancient Covenant. Nor can she forget that she draws sustenance from the root of that well-cultivated olive tree onto which have been grafted the wild shoots, the Gentiles (Rom. 11: 17-24)." Other than the exclusivist substitutional thinking, *Nostra Aetate* also draws attention to the continuity of Judaism and Christianity. In this way, the document tries to overcome the problem of *supersessionism*.

The significance and meaning of the declaration of the ecclesiastical document *Nostra Aetate* in 1965 cannot be underestimated. Rightly, it is spoken of as a turning point in the history of Jewish-Christian relations. This document holds massive symbolic importance. It ushers in a new era for the relationship between the Church and Israel. Despite the undeniable significance of *Nostra Aetate*, a critical reading demonstrates that the text still contains some elements referring to substitution theology. For instance, the text refers to the salvation of the Church which is mysteriously "foreshadowed by the chosen people's exodus from the land of bondage," and to "Jerusalem [that] did not recognize the time of her visitation," and to the Church as "the new people of God." In this perspective, the document *Nostra Aetate* illustrates how, during the Second Vatican Council, the Church still wrestled with the relationship vis-à-vis the Jewish people and particularly with its ancient substitutive self-understanding.[9]

In this contribution, we will investigate how the Catholic Church further developed its relationship with Israel after the publication of *Nostra Aetate* and its attempts to overcome substitution theology. To that end, we will focus on the work of Cardinal Joseph Ratzinger,

[9] All quotations in the following paragraph are taken from the Second Vatican Council document *Nostra Aetate*: *Declaration on the Relation of the Church to non-Christian Religions*, October 28th, 1965, nr. 4.

now pope Benedict XVI. We consider his position, as former prefect of the Congregation for the Doctrine of the Faith, as particularly representative for the Catholic position today and, also for Jewish-Christian relations in the future, now that he is pope. Special attention will be paid to the book Ratzinger published about this subject in 1999, *Many Religions — One Covenant: Israel, the Church, and the World*.[10] In this work, Ratzinger speaks in positive terms about the reconciliation among Jews and Christians, and he emphasizes the lasting role of the Jewish people.[11] At the same time, Ratzinger defends the value of the Hebrew Bible. In *Many Religions — One Covenant*, this positive appreciation is translated into a theology of fulfillment. The Church does not replace Israel in God's salvific plan but rather professes that the partial truths, which God revealed to the Jewish people, are transcended, fulfilled, and completed in Jesus. The unique Christ event is the climax of God's salvific action in history and God's revelation has achieved its fullness in Jesus Christ. Jesus Christ fulfills what God had initiated with Israel. However, we will argue that this fulfillment thinking underlying Ratzinger's theology causes the relations among Jews and Christians to default into a kind of paradox that was already obvious in *Nostra Aetate*. On the one hand it is stated that the first covenant has never been revoked, on the other hand it is constantly suggested that that the fist covenant has merely a preparatory function towards the new covenant God has made through Christ. In *Many Religions — One Covenant*, Ratzinger not only recognizes this paradoxical theological situation, but he also accepts it both as a believer and as a theologian. In this perspective, Ratzinger speaks of an unsolvable paradox.

---

[10] Joseph Ratzinger, *Many Religions — One Covenant: Israel, the Church, and the World* (San Francisco, CA: Ignatius Press, 1999).

[11] *Ibid.*, 103. "The Jews must remain as the first proprietors of Holy Scripture with respect to us, in order to establish a testimony to the world."

In this contribution, we will demonstrate that this paradoxical situation is not unproblematic. Firstly, Ratzinger does not entirely succeed in putting an end to replacement thinking. In our opinion, the reason is that it does not become clear how 'fulfillment' can be sufficiently distinguished from replacement. Fulfillment thinking is characterized by an ongoing tension translated into thinking patterns such as promise-fulfillment, unfinished-finished, imperfect-perfect, etc. Admittedly, in these schemes the focus is not on the substitution of Israel by the Church, but on the fulfillment of the first covenant by the second, even though this fulfillment is usually considered in an eschatological way. However, the question remains, what is the lasting significance of the first covenant if a more complete second covenant exists. Theologically speaking, what is the value of God's first covenant with Israel in light of the choice of God to make a new, unconditional, and more complete covenant through Christ? Put differently, to confirm that the *old covenant* has never been revoked[12] is of little value as long as no theological reason is provided for the existence of Judaism after the coming of Christ.[13] It is precisely this question that cannot be answered sufficiently within the fulfillment thinking. Because fulfillment thinking does not sufficiently recognize the intrinsic — and as such lasting — value and significance of Judaism, the Catholic Church has difficulty in defintively detaching herself from *substitution thinking*. According to us, *fulfillment thinking* remains kindred to *replacement thinking*.

[12] Pope John Paul II has confirmed this lasting significance of Israel in his speech to the Jewish community of West Germany in Mainz on November 17th, 1980. He there spoke of "The people of God of the Old Covenant, which has never been revoked."

[13] Mary C. Boys, "The Covenant in Contemporary Ecclesial Documents," *Two Faiths, One Covenant: Jewish Identity and Christian Identity in the Presence of the Other*, ed. E. B. Korn & J. Pawlikowski (Lanham, MD: Rowman & Littlefield, 2005) 81-110, 82.

Ratzinger's conclusion that the relation between the Church and Israel is paradoxical has much to do with the clearly inclusivist parameters within which he places the relation between Church and Israel. Inclusivism — applied to Jewish-Christian dialogue — tries to balance both rejection and acceptance of Israel's role in God's salvific plan. The Church confirms Israel's intrinsic value but always within the borders of particular Christian *a priori's*, such as the uniqueness of Jesus as the universal savior on God's behalf. Through Christ all people — including the Jews — will be saved. Between Judaism and Christianity, there exists no such thing as soteriological equality.

Secondly, in this contribution we will illustrate how this theological paradox puts increasing pressure on the relations between the Church and Israel and interreligious dialogue. In 2008 this was demonstrated in the controversy surrounding the New Good Friday prayer commisioned by pope Benedict XVI. At heart, this controversy revolves around ambigiuty, because of the ongoing failure to bring theological appreciation of Israel in God's salvific plan and the trouble Catholic theology has in shedding light on its relation to *substitution thinking*. It is our thesis that theology does not do any good by accepting the abovementioned paradox as *unsolvable*. We do believe that this paradox implies a hindrance to the progress of Jewish-Christian dialogue. A theology that keeps repeating mantra-like that Israel is *dear to God* and that the *old* covenant has a lasting significance in God's salvific plan, and yet at the same time continues to pray for the conversion of the Jewish people to Christ — as is the case in the new Good Friday prayer — such a theology lacks authenticity and coherence in the eyes of many. Precisely this lack of authenticity and coherence puts an increasing pressure on contemporary Jewish-Christian dialogue. Nowadays, we hear often speak of stagnation or a crisis in Jewish-Christian relations or, what is worse, that it is, simply passé.

'MANY RELIGIONS — ONE COVENANT. ISRAEL, THE CHURCH, AND THE WORLD': FULFILMENT OR REPLACEMENT?

In his book *Many Religions — One Covenant*, Ratzinger formulates the central theological question to Christians regarding contemporary theology of Jewish-Christian relationship in clear-cut terms:

> Do confession of Jesus of Nazareth as the Son of the Living God and faith in the Cross as the redemption of mankind contain an implicit condemnation of the Jews as stubborn and blind, as guilty of the death of the Son of God?[14]

Concerning the last part of the question, Ratzinger refers to *Nostra Aetate* art. 4, that mentions that "the report of Jesus' trial cannot substantiate a charge of collective Jewish guilt." "All sinners were the authors of Christ's Passion."[15] In the first part of the question, Ratzinger approaches Jesus as "the promised shoot of Judah," who has come to reconcile Israel and the nations, in the Kingdom of God. In Jesus, the history of Israel becomes the history of the whole humanity.[16] The inclusive mission of Jesus unites Jews and gentiles in one single people in completion of Scripture.[17]

The notion of *fulfillment* best summarizes Ratzinger's position . This concept locates Jesus primarily in line with the Jewish tradition. He fulfills the universal promise of the Scriptures.[18] Here, Jesus and Israel's Holy Scriptures appear as inextricably bound.[19]

> Through him whom the Church believes to be Jesus Christ and Son of God, the God of Israel has become the God of the nations,

---

[14] Ratzinger, *Many Religions — One Covenant*, 23.
[15] *Ibid.*, 42.
[16] *Ibid.*, 27.
[17] *Ibid.*, 26.
[18] *Ibid.*
[19] *Ibid.*, 28.

fulfilling the prophecy that the Servant of God would bring the light of this God to the nations.[20] [Italics ours]

This concept of *fulfillment* clearly places Jesus in continuity with the old covenant. This focus on the continuity is confirmed by the following quotation from Ratzinger's article *The Heritage of Abraham — the Gift of Christmas*: "the New Testament consciousness of God, which finds its climax in the Johannine definition that 'God is Love' (Jn 4:16) does not contradict the past, but rather serves as a summary of all of salvation history, which initially had Israel as its central figure."[21] For Ratzinger, it follows that, on the one hand, the Church should cherish a great gratitude towards Israel since she owes her faith to her Jewish brothers and sisters, who, "despite the hardships of their own history, have held on to faith in this God right up to the present, and who witness to it in the sight of those peoples who, lacking knowledge of the one God, "dwell in darkness and in the shadow of death" (Lu. 1:79)."[22]

On the other hand, Ratzinger also notices a possible theological appreciation for Jesus by the Jewish communities. Even if it is impossible for Israel to regard Jesus as the Son of God in the way Christians do, it should still be possible for them, according to Ratzinger, "to see Jesus as the Servant of God who has come to carry the divine light to all nations."[23] Jesus does not abrogate the *Old Covenant*.[24] On the contrary, Jesus is the perfect fulfillment of what is predicted in the *Old Covenant*[25] about the servant of God.

Nevertheless, for Christians this fulfillment means much more than a mere continuation; it signifies a broadening and universalizing of

[20] Ratzinger, *Many Religions — One Covenant*, 18-19.
[21] Joseph Ratzinger, "The Heritage of Abraham — The Gift of Christmas," *L'Osservatore Romano*, 29 December 2000, 2.
[22] *Ibid.*, 2.
[23] Ratzinger, *Many Religions — One Covenant*, 104.
[24] *Ibid.*, 62.
[25] *Ibid.*, 32.

the history of Israel. Ratzinger criticizes the contemporary representations of "Jesus as a Jewish teacher, who did not go beyond what was possible in the Jewish tradition."[26] In the fulfillment process, the Old Testament is at the same time "renewed"[27] by Jesus, "transformed,"[28] and "brought to its deepest meaning."[29] Through Jesus, it is God himself who fundamentally reinterprets the Law and who shows Christians that only now the Law finds its actually intended significance:

> When Jesus offers the cup to the disciples and says, "This is the blood of the covenant," the words of Sinai are heightened to a staggering realism, and at the same time we begin to see a totally unexpected depth in them. What takes place here is both spiritualization and the greatest possible realism.[30]

It is clear, however, that this use of 'fulfillment' in expressions like 'renewal', 'reinterpretation', 'transformation', 'intensifying', and 'deepening' creates quite some tension in Ratzinger's analysis — a tension to which we already referred at the beginning of this article and of which traces can also be found in *Nostra Aetate*. On the one hand, Ratzinger stresses that in the Christological movement, where all nations become brothers and receivers of the promises of the chosen People, "not one iota of it [the Old Testament] is being lost"[31] and that this new perspective in Jesus does not imply "the abolishment of the special mission of Israel."[32] Instead it concerns a 'fulfillment':

> All cultic ordinances of the Old Testament are seen to be taken up into his death and brought to their deepest meaning ... The universalizing of the Torah by Jesus ... preserves the unity of cult and

---

[26] Ratzinger, *Many Religions — One Covenant*, 23.
[27] *Ibid.*, 62.
[28] *Ibid.*, 39.
[29] *Ibid.*, 32.
[30] *Ibid.*, 60.
[31] *Ibid.*, 41.
[32] *Ibid.*, 27.

ethos... The entire cult is bound together in the Cross, indeed, for the first time has become fully real.[33]

On the other hand, the emphasis on the newness of Jesus implies, at times, that the Sinai covenant "within God's providential rule... is a stage that has its own allotted period of time."[34] The Sinai covenant thus seems to have only a conditional and as such temporary significance. Several times throughout the book, Ratzinger's analysis refers explicitly to the terminology of replacement theology. He argues that replacement theology is already present in the First Testament. The new covenant which God himself establishes, is already present in the faith of Israel (Jeremiah 11).

> God, according to the Prophet, will *replace* the broken Sinai covenant with a New Covenant that cannot be broken: this is because it will not confront man in the form of a book or a stone tablet but will be inscribed on his heart. The *conditional* covenant, which depended on man's faithful observance of the Law, is *replaced* by the *unconditional* covenant in which God binds himself irrevocably.[35] [Italics ours]

At this point in his book, Ratzinger nowhere says that the covenant has been replaced by the flesh and blood of the risen Christ. But, by referring in the same study to the theology of the new covenant in the First Testament which replaces the broken covenant and to the idea of the 'fulfillment' in Christ the replacement theology gets a Christological plausibility, especially because Ratzinger never makes an explicit distinction between 'fulfillment' and 'replacement'.

---

[33] Ratzinger, *Many Religions — One Covenant*, 41.
[34] *Ibid.*, 68.
[35] *Ibid.*, 63-64.

This confusion becomes clear again when Ratzinger writes the following:

> Thus the Sinai covenant is indeed *superseded*. But once what was provisional in it has been *swept away*, we see what is truly definitive in it. So the expectation of the New Covenant, which becomes clearer and clearer as the history of Israel unfolds, does not conflict with the Sinai covenant; rather, it *fulfils* the dynamic expectation found in that very covenant.[36] [italics ours]

This quote illustrates how, for Ratzinger 'fulfillment' of the 'Old Covenant' immediately implies 'replacement'. He even speaks of the Sinai covenant as being swept away. In this perspective, several theological questions ask for an answer. What can be the remaining role and significance of the first covenant in God's salvific plan? Does God's covenant with Israel not suffice for the salvation of the Jewish people? To put it sharply, are the Jewish people saved through Christ or in and through "the never revoked covenant" (John Paul II) which God sealed with them on Mount Sinai? Do the Jews have to convert to Christ to enter into God's final Kingdom?

Ratzinger acknowledges that his theological analysis ends with a paradoxical conclusion which, according to him, can only find a solution in an eschatological perspective.

> It follows, therefore, that the figure of Christ both links and separates Israel and the Church. It is not within our power to overcome this separation, but it keeps both of us to the path that leads to the One who comes. To that extend the relationship between us must not be one of enmity.[37]

In fact, this is the conclusion of Ratzinger's approach, namely that 'separation' and 'reconciliation' among Jews and Christians are

---

[36] Ratzinger, *Many Religions — One Covenant*, 70-71.
[37] *Ibid.*, 106.

intertwined in what he calls a "virtually insolvable paradox."[38]
By reconciling himself to this paradox, Ratzinger also provides theological plausibility to the 'confusion' between 'replacement' and
fulfillment'.

According to Ratzinger, this situation is livable when it is put in —
some will say postponed to[39] — an eschatological perspective. Positive about such an 'eschatological solution' is the acknowledgement
that even today the Church does not dispose of the fullness of the
truth and that as such, analogous to the Jewish people, the Church
lives in the same expectation of the definitive salvation. Such an eschatological perspective stresses the mysterious character of the truth and
salvation and thus it confirms that Israel and the Church find themselves in a similar situation. Both the Church and Israel live in the
hopeful expectation that God will bring justice. "The Church too
awaits the Messiah. She already knows him, yet he has still to reveal
his glory."

In light of the long history of exclusivist anti-Judaism, it is
important to mention that this 'eschatologizing' clearly recognizes
that *not the Church* but *rather God* brings salvation to all people.
In other words, the Church renounces its role as being God's sin-
gular instrument for salvation. This is confirmed by Cardinal Walter Kasper: "The Church simply cannot do this [setting itself up as
God's only instrument for salvation]. The Church places the when
and how entirely in God's hands. God only can bring the Kingdom
of God, in which the world will know eschatological peace and the
whole of Israel will be saved."[40]

---

[38] Ratzinger, *Many Religions — One Covenant*, 40.

[39] Manfred Vogel, "The Problem of Dialogue Between Judaism and Christianity," *Journal of Ecumenical Studies* 4 (1967) 684-699, 689, nr. 2.

[40] Walter Kasper, "Il Cardinale Kasper e la missione verso gli ebrei. Risponde
alle critiche del Venerdì Santo per gli ebrei," *Osservatore Romano,*10 April, 2008.

To Ratzinger, this eschatological delay is 'good enough', since it can prevent enmity and violence among Christians and Jews. The special mission of Israel is not abolished by Jesus.

We also believe that Christians find themselves in a paradoxical situation, forty years after *Nostra Aetate*. A situation that in a certain sense is characteristic of the very text of *Nostra Aetate*, which is caught in a tension between continuity and discontinuity with the Jewish tradition, between separation and reconciliation, between fulfillment and replacement theology. However, we ask ourselves if it is, theologically speaking, opportune to accept this paradox as unsolvable. After all, we think that the tension between 'replacement' and 'fulfillment' is quite problematic, even when placed in an eschatological perspective. It is not evident for Christians-in-dialogue to engage in a real encounter with the Jewish other when these Christians are confronted with an irresolvable paradox. In the long run, this situation will not serve the Jewish-Christian relations as such.

Even though we find many Jewish dialogue partners to be satisfied with 'the eschatological solution' and that, at first sight, they show little interest to participate in a discussion they consider an internal Christian one, it has recently been proven that this "irresolvable paradox" (Ratzinger) does indeed bear consequences that complicate the relationship between the Church and Israel. We particularly think about the controversy that arose in Jewish-Christian circles following the *motu proprio* (a letter on personal authority of the pope, outside the curia) in which pope Benedict XVI gave permission for a broader use of the Tridentine rite. It is appropriate to take a closer look at the controversy that emerged as a result of this *motu propio* and the reviewed Good Friday prayer, precisely because this commotion illustrates that the aforementioned paradox in the position of Ratzinger — a tension characteristic for the Catholic Church's attitude vis-à-vis

Israel — becomes a source of many problems. According to us, this controversy is the logical outcome of Ratzingers particular inclusivist theological vision. This inclusivist vision is typified by a tension between, on the one hand, a desire to do justice to the idea of the "never revoked covenant" (Rom 11:29; John Paul II) and, on the other, a strong Christocentrism. Actually, on the pastoral level Ratzinger, now as pope, does exactly what he has done on the level of his systematic theology; there is continuity in both his book and his prayer.

THE CONTROVERSY CONCERNING THE GOOD FRIDAY PRAYER: A NEW OBSTACLE IN THE JEWISH-CHRISTIAN DIALOGUE

The Tridentine rite is the liturgy introduced by pope Paul V as standard for the Catholic Mass in 1570. Up until the Second Vatican Council this rite remained the norm, albeit in the 1962 version of the Roman Missal. This Tridentine rite, sometimes referred to as the *old Ordo Missae*, has been replaced by the *new Ordo Missae* by pope Paul VI in 1970 according to the liturgical renewal that followed the Second Vatican Council and that counts as standard for the entire Catholic Church ever since. The *old Ordo Missae*, however, has never been abolished officially. A small minority of rather traditionalistic and conservative Catholics stuck to the old Tridentine rite even after the Council. The old Tridentine rite has been formally rehabilitated through the *motu proprio Summorum Pontificum* dated July 7th, 2007. After this papal initiative, the Tridentine rite is considered an *extraordinary* form of the Latin rite, whereas the 1970 Roman Missal (the *new Ordo Missae*) remains the *ordinary* form or expression.

Even though, at first sight, this decision involves a mere *internal Christian matter*, this papal initiative ignites particular concern and irritation among Jews.[41] Many Catholics as well raise questions over the desirability and appropriateness of this *motu proprio*.[42] Especially Catholics who are engaged in Jewish-Christian dialogue experience this *motu proprio* as a step back vis-à-vis the openness breathed by the Second Vatican Council.[43] It was particularly feared that the revaluation of this *old Ordo Missae* would lead to a reintroduction of the classic Good Friday prayer, including the 1948 missal in which is prayed for the unreliable — [the original text uses the word] *perfidious* — Jews:

> Let us pray also for the perfidious Jews: that Almighty God may remove the veil from their hearts; so that they too may acknowledge Jesus Christ our Lord. Almighty and eternal God, who dost not exclude from thy mercy even Jewish faithlessness: hear our prayers, which we offer for the blindness of that people; that acknowledging the light of thy Truth, which is Christ, they may be delivered from their darkness. Through the same Lord Jesus Christ, who lives and reigns with thee in the unity of the Holy Spirit, God, for ever and ever. Amen.

In light of the long history of ecclesiastic anti-Judaism, the wary Jewish attitude towards the *old Ordo Missae* and this Good Friday prayer is perfectly understandable. For centuries, Good Friday has been the most dangerous day of the year for Jews.[44] On this day Christians commemorate the suffering and death of Jesus Christ. Not infrequently, this liturgical memorial led to spontaneous or

[41] David Rosen, "American Jewish Committee Seeks Clarification on Latin Mass;" www.sidic.org.

[42] John Pawlikowski, "Praying for the Jews," *Commonweal*, March 14, 2008.

[43] Hans-Peter Heinz & Henry Brandt, "A New Burden on Christian-Jewish Relations: Statement of the Discussion Group 'Jews and Christians' of the Central Committee of German Catholics on the Good Friday Prayer 'For the Jews' in the Extraordinary Rite Version of 2008."

[44] Judith Banki, "Praying for the Jews. Two Views on the New Good Friday Prayer," *Commonweal*, March 14, 2008, 12.

even orchestrated outbursts of anger against the Jewish population, who were thought to be collectively guilty for the death of Christ.[45]

Official Catholic sources reacted with the following, threefold message against Jewish and Catholic anxiety.[46] Firstly, the observation was made that Benedict XVI's *motu proprio* concerned the 1962 version in which the problematic concept 'perfidis Judaeis' was already expunged. Secondly, it was emphasized that, despite the pope's *motu proprio*, the Roman missal of 1970 remains the qualifying missal for the ordinary rite. Hence, there is no question about some sort of general return to the Tridentine rite. Finally, on January 28th 2008, the pope made known that he intended to write a new prayer in which he would take into account the sensitivities felt on the Jewish side. The reviewed version of the Good Friday prayer is a reformulation of the 1962 missal's Good Friday prayer.

Despite the insistence of various Jewish and even Catholic groups, the pope does not let the 1970 Good Friday prayer, that breathed the positive dialogical spirit of Vatican II, *enter into* the Roman missal of 1962.[47] The reviewed Good Friday prayer, as presented by pope Benedict XVI, does not succeed in taking away the troubling issues raised by both Jews and Catholics.[48] The new Good Friday prayer lacks the positive language and insights of the postconciliar liturgy.[49] Indeed, the comparison between the 1970 Good Friday prayer current up until now, and the new Good Friday prayer

[45] Cf. The teaching of the deicide.

[46] Vatican Secretariat of State, "The new Prayer for the Jews for the 1962 edition of the Roman Missal — Communiqué," April 4, 2008; www.sidic.org.

[47] See among others the letter of John Pawlikowski, president of the 'International Council of Christians and Jews', to cardinal Walter Kasper, Pontifical Commission for the Relations with the Jews'; www.sidic.org.

[48] Abraham Foxman, "Anti-Defamation League statement about the Papal Motu Proprio on the 1962 Missal"; www.sidic.org.

[49] Francis Rocca, "Pope Tweaks Prayer to Address Jewish Concerns," *Christian Century*, March 11, 2008, 18-19, 19.

(2008) makes clear that the Benedict XVI prayer is a step back-wards compared to the prayer by pope Paul VI and the symbolic actions and sayings of John Paul II.[50] In this way, we now have two authorized Good Friday prayers in the Catholic Church today which, as will become clear later in this article, breathe a different theological spirit:

The revised Good Friday Prayer (2008)	The Good Friday Prayer (1970)
"Let us pray also for the Jews. That our Lord and God may enlighten their hearts, that they may acknowledge Jesus Christ as the savior of all men.	"Let us pray for the Jewish people, the first to hear the word of God, that they may continue to grow in the love of his name and in faithfulness to his covenant.
Almighty, ever living God, who wills that all men would be saved and come to the knowledge of the truth, graciously grant that all Israel may be saved when the fullness of the nations enter into Your Church.	Almighty and eternal God, long ago you gave your promise to Abraham and his posterity. Listen to your Church as we pray that the people you first made your own may arrive at the fullness of redemption.
Through Christ Our Lord. Amen."	We ask this through Christ our Lord. Amen."

Even though this new Good Friday prayer cannot be compared to the 1948 version, it does not succeed in taking away the Jewish — and Christian — displeasure entirely. There are several reasons for this.

[50] Heinz & Brandt, "A New Burden on Christian-Jewish Relations."

The 1970 missal not only renounces any negative attitude towards the Jews but integrates the theological-liturgical insights of the Second Vatican Council as well. This version of the Good Friday prayer speaks of the Jewish people in clearly positive terms and it does recognize the soteriological priority of the Jewish people in God's salvific plan. God has turned Himself to the Jews first. The Jewish people is the chosen people that "God elevates in love for Gods name." The new Good Friday prayer of 2008 passes over this post-conciliar insight. The Jews' never-ending love of God is not mentioned any longer.

In the Good Friday prayer of the 1970 missal, the Church renounces its claim to pray for the conversion of the Jews to Christ. According to this version of the Good Friday prayer, the Jews are already on the way to salvation. Here, the Church does not speak about the acknowledgement of Christ as a condition to achieve salvation. Apparently, the Church relies on the fact that the faith in the union between the Jewish people and God will bring the Jews towards salvation;[51] moreover, the 1970 prayer for the Jews mirrors the prayer of the Church for itself. In this way, the Church also indicates that it has not yet arrived at complete salvation itself. With this, the Church recognizes that *not She* but *God only* determines the how and when of salvation. For both the Jewish people and the Church, the completion of salvation is placed in an explicit eschatological perspective.

In contrast to the 1970 missal, the new Good Friday prayer (2008) does appeal for the conversion of the Jews to Christ, the Saviour on God's behalf, of all people. Even though the word 'conversion' is not mentioned in the text, it is implied in the petition for 'enlightenment' for the Jews. Moreover, this prayer for the 'enlightenment' of the Jews gives the impression that the Jewish

---

[51] Heinz & Brandt, "A New Burden on Christian-Jewish Relations."

people find themselves in 'darkness' today. Here, Judaism takes particularly offence at this appeal for conversion. First of all, through this call for conversion the place of the Jewish people in God's salvific plan is placed in a privative scheme — the Jewish people lack the truth that has been revealed in Christ. Moreover, this call to enlightenment recalls reminiscences to the older Good Friday prayer of 1948, in which it is said about the Jews that they are blinded and that they lack the light of the Christian truth.[52]

Probably Benedict XVI will not share this critical analysis. After all, the new Good Friday prayer says nothing new but only speaks openly about what the Church has always considered self-evident. With this prayer, Benedict XVI confirms that Christ fulfils what God had begun in Israel. The Jewish people will come to the fullness of the truth only when they turn to Christ. Actually, this means that Jews need to convert to Christ and hence become Christians. Jews are considered "potential Christians."[53] In this way, we run into the abovementioned tension between fulfillment and replacement. The call to conversion implicitly means that the election of the Jews as the chosen people and their particular mission have actually lost their significance after the coming of Christ. Fulfillment and replacement are closely tied. Christ not only fulfils what God has started with Israel; the Church also replaces the Jewish people who, as such, have no lasting meaning and role in God's salvific plan. There is no longer an engagement with the words of John-Paul II about the lasting meaning of the covenant which has "never been revoked" and which will never be revoked.

---

[52] See above.

[53] See Byron L. Sherwin, "John Paul II's Catholic Theology of Judaism," *John Paul II and Interreligious Dialogue*, ed. Sherwin & Kasimow, 141.

According to Walter Kasper, the call to conversion of the
Jewish people should be put into an eschatological perspective.[54]
Pope Benedict XVI has supported this perspective.[55] The fact is,
however, that in the new Good Friday prayer this eschatological
perspective cannot be explicitly found. This arouses the suggestion
that the Church, in its missionary activities, is also to direct itself
to the Jewish people as well. This suggestion is reinforced by the
use of the various Latin verb conjugations and tenses: the prayer
uses the present participle (participium praesens,) whereas the
"neo-Vulgate" translation[56] makes use of a future conjunctive
(conjunctivus futuri.)[57] This can create the impression that the
Jews should recognize Jesus as Savior of all people now already.
And even the eschatological perspective remains problematic,
because it places the Jews in a privative scheme that is difficult to
reconcile with the concept of the "never revoked covenant" of
John Paul II.

It is also striking is also that in the new Good Friday prayer the
conversion takes a strong ecclesiological direction: the Jews will
enter into the Church. In the letter to the Romans 11, to which this
missal alludes, there is no reference made to an 'entrance' into the

[54] Walter Kasper, "Il Cardinale Kasper e la missione verso gli ebrei. Risponde
alle critiche del Venerdì Santo per gli ebrei."

[55] "As Cardinal Kasper has clearly explained, the new Oremus et pro Iudaeis
is not intended to promote proselytism towards the Jews and opens up an eschatological perspective. Christians however cannot but bear witness to their faith in
full and total respect for the freedom of others, and this leads them also to pray
that all will come to recognize Christ." See "Letter of Card. Tarcisio Bertone in
Response to Concerns on the revised Good Friday prayer", May 15, 2008;
www.sidic.org.

[56] The Neo-Vulgate, also known as the 'Vulgata Paulus', came into being
under pope Paul VI (1963-1978) and was promulgated under pope Johannes
Paul II in 1979.

[57] Katholieke Raad voor Israël, "Het Goede Vrijdag gebed voor de Joden in
de Tridentijnse ritus 2008," www.kri-web.nl.

Church, but rather of an entrance into the *mystery*. As a consequence, the new Good Friday prayer arouses (nasty) reminiscences of the ecclesiocentric exclusivism that has determined the soteriological position of the Church for so long. "No salvation outside the Church." Once again, we detect that the fulfillment concept blends into the old replacement concept: the Jews need to be enlightened. Christ brings salvation — also for the Jewish people — and the Church replaces Israel. Hence, the abovementioned annoyance of Jews and Christians about the new Good Friday prayer is quite understandable:

> Like his predecessor, Benedict XVI has reached out to the Jewish community in friendship on several occasions. This newly issued prayer for the conversion of the Jews may be intended to restate the fundamental message of the church regarding the universal salvific uniqueness of Christ. But for many Jews the very word "conversion" will recall campaigns, not prayerful hopes: the Crusades, the forced disputations and sermons, the expulsions, the Inquisition, the ghettos.[58]

CONCLUSION

Pope Benedict XVI's concern for the success of the Jewish-Christian dialogue is intellectually sharp and challenging. However, the controversy around the renewed Good Friday prayer makes clear that the tension between *replacement* and *fulfillment*, the intrinsic value of Judaism and Christ as universal savior, forms a hindrance to the Jewish-Christian dialogue. The *confusing theory* of the theological interpretation brings about serious consequences for the

---

[58] Banki, "Praying for the Jews: Two Views on the New Good Friday Prayer," 12.

practice of Judeo-Christian conversations. The question of the role and significance of the Jewish people in God's salvific plan is not a mere theoretical problem bit it contains a clear pastoral aspect as well.[59] The way in which this question is answered or remains unanswered will also determine how Christians relate to the Jewish people.[60] *Lex orandi, lex credendi.*

We cannot escape the impression that Benedict XVI is confined to the limitations of classic theological thinking patterns; patterns in which the relationship between the Church and the Jewish people took shape since the Second Vatican Council. We ask ourselves the question if it is not about time for Catholic theology to thoroughly reconsider the relation between the Church and the Jewish people. This implies, however, the willingness to become detached from certain theological presuppositions. Right now, Christian theology too often departs from dogmatic *a priori's* that limit any possible outcome of the Jewish-Christian dialogue right from the start. The result is a Christian theology of Judaism too loosely formulated from an interreligious dialogue — that is, a theology which lets itself be fed by the encounter with the other. When we turn to the Jewish people in dialogue, it is of vital importance that Christians (and Jews as well) create space for an imaginative theology which dares to follow new roads past the beaten paths. Only than will it be possible to give

---

[59] The bond between the theologies of the religions on the one hand and the practice of interreligious dialogue on the other can be determined already from the very beginning of this theological discipline—this is around the Second Vatican Council. In this perspective, the conciliar document *Nostra Aetate*, the Declaration on the Relation of the Church to non-Christian Religions, set the trend by developing some major theological initiatives for the promotion of relations between the Church and the other religions.

[60] Andreas Eckerstorfer, *Kirche in der postmodernen Welt: Der Beitrag George Lindbecks zu einer neuen Verhältnisbestimmung* (Innsbruck: Tyrolia, 2001) 135.

shape in a theologically responsible way to a thesis in Ratzinger's earlier work that the "Old Testament is... open to both ways" (Ratzinger).[61]

---

[61] Ratzinger, *Milestones: Memoirs 1927-1977* (San Francisco, CA: Ignatius Press, 1998) 53-54. "I have come to the realization that Judaism (which strictly speaking, began with the end of the formation of the Canon, that is, in the first century after Christ) and the Christian faith described in the New Testament are two ways of appropriating Israel's Scriptures, two ways that in the end are determined by the position one assumes with regard to the figure of Jesus of Nazareth. The Scripture we today call Old Testament is in and of itself open to both ways."

PERSONALIA

Mary Boys, Skinner and McAlpin Professor of Practical Theology at Union Theological Seminary in New York, U.S.A.

Leo Declerck, priest of de diocese of Bruges. He obtained a master in Philosophy (1959) and in Theology (1963) at the Pontifical Gregorian University of Rome. He was professor at the Seminary of Bruges (1966-1967), president of the Secretary of the Belgian conference of Bishops (1967-1972) and vicar-general of the diocese of Bruges (1972-1996). He is now vicar-general emeritus.

Mathijs Lamberigts, full Professor, former dean of the Faculty of theology (2000-2008), K.U.Leuven. He teaches Church history, focusing both on Augustine and the Pelagian controversy and on history of Vatican II.

David Meyer, was rabbi at the Liberal Synagogue Bet Hillel for five years. He is now the rabbi at the Brighton New Synagogue in the South of England.

Marianne Moyaert, postdoctoral researcher (National Fund for Scientific Research, Belgium), Faculty of Theology, K.U.Leuven. Her research focuses on the impact of vulnerable faith commitments on interreligious dialogue.

John T. Pawlikowski, OSM, priest of the Servite order, professor of Social Ethics and Director of Catholic-Jewish Studies at the Catholic Theological Union, part of the ecumenical cluster of theological schools at the University of Chicago. He is the President of the International Council of Christians & Jews (ICCJ) and its Abrahamic Form.

Didier Pollefeyt, full professor, vice-dean for education, Faculty of Theology, K.U.Leuven. He teaches Jewish-Christian Relations, catechetics and religious education. He is a member of the Belgian National Catholic Commission for the Religious Relations with the Jews, the Institutum Iudaicum, the Council for Christians and Jews in Belgium.

Simon Schoon, Minister of the Reformed Church, Gouda, and Professor of Jewish-Christian Relations, Theological University, Kampen, Netherlands.